THE
Oklahoma Basic
INTELLIGENCE
TEST

THE
Oklahoma Basic
INTELLIGENCE
TEST

▼ ▼ ▼

New and Collected Elementary, Epistolary,
Autobiographical, and Oratorical Choctologies

D.L. Birchfield

THE GREENFIELD REVIEW PRESS

FRANK WATERS MEMORIAL SERIES, Volume #2

Publication of this volume has been made possible, in part, through a grant from The Bay Foundation to support this second in a series of volumes of prose writing by Native American Authors. This series, named in honor of the memory of Frank Waters, consists of the annual winners of The North American Native Authors First Book Award for Prose.

ISBN 0-912678-97-6

Library of Congress Card Catalog Number: 98-72550

Cover and Interior Design and
Composition by Sans Serif Typesetters
Saline, Michigan

Distributed by The Talman Co. Inc.
131 Spring Street
N.Y., N.Y.
(212) 431-7175 Fax (212) 431-7215

Contents

IV.

Acknowledgments

Many of the items in this volume have appeared in *Roundup* (Encampment, WY: Western Writers of America); *The Raven Chronicles: A Multicultural Journal of Literature, Art, and The Spoken Word* (Seattle, WA); *Blue Dawn, Red Earth: New Native American Storytellers* (NY: Doubleday/Anchor, 1996); *Absolute* (Oklahoma City Community College); *ELF: Eclectic Literary Forum* (Tonawanda, NY); *Durable Breath: Contemporary Native American Poetry* (Anchorage, AK: Salmon Run Press, 1994); *Gatherings: The En'owkin Journal of First North American Peoples* (Penticton, BC, Canada: Theytus Books, 1993 and 1997); *ARIEL: A Review of International Literature in English* (University of Calgary); *Camp Crier* (Oklahoma City Native American Center); *Turtle Quarterly* (Niagara Falls, NY: Native American Center For The Living Arts); *Spirit Talk: A Publication In Celebration Of Indian Culture* (Browning, MT); *Studies In American Indian Literatures* (University of Richmond, VA: Association for the Study of American Indian Literatures); *The Four Directions: American Indian Literary Quarterly* (Tellico Plains, TN); *News From Indian Country* (Hayward, WI); and *Bishinik* (Durant, OK: Choctaw Nation of Oklahoma).

Introductory
Choctologies
▼ ▼ ▼ ▼ ▼ ▼ ▼ ▼ ▼

Elementary Choctology

▼ ▼ ▼ ▼ ▼ ▼ ▼ ▼ ▼ ▼ ▼ ▼ ▼ ▼ ▼ ▼

The new governor of French Louisiana meets the Choctaws:

> "It seems to me that they are true to their plighted faith. But we must be the same in our transactions with them. They are men who reflect, and who have more logic and precision in their reasoning than it is commonly thought." —Kerleric, 1753

One year later:

> "I am sufficiently acquainted with the Choctaws to know that they are covetous, lying, and treacherous. So that I keep on my guard without showing it." —Kerleric, 1754

Choctology 101

▼▼▼▼▼▼▼▼▼▼▼▼▼▼▼▼

In the long chronicle of human endeavor, great civilizations have arisen along the lower reaches of the great rivers of the world; thus, the Tigris-Euphrates gave us the civilization of Mesopotamia, the Nile gave us the civilization of Egypt, the Yangtze gave us the civilization of China, and the Mississippi gave us the civilization of the Choctaws.

It happened like this: At a time when there were no people in the world, a hole opened in the earth near the sacred mound of *Nanih Wayih*. From out of this hole emerged a people, who greeted the sun by draping themselves on the bushes to dry off in its life-giving warmth. Then they went off to find their homes. They would become the people who live the furthest from *Nanih Wayih*, so far away that they scarcely remember the sacred mother mound.

Next, another people emerged from the hole, and after they had dried themselves off in the sun, they, too, went off to find their homes. They would also become a people who live a great distance from *Nanih Wayih*, not quite so far away as the first group, but far enough away that they would have almost as much difficulty remembering how to be Indians.

For a long time people continued emerging from the hole, and drying themselves off in the sun, and going off to find their homes, settling ever closer to *Nanih Wayih*, and looking, and speaking, and behaving more and more the way Indians ought to look, and speak, and behave.

Finally, when the earth was nearly filled up with people, the oldest people of all emerged from the hole, who had waited patiently for the others to go off and find their place in the world. These were the Choctaws. For their patience and generosity, they were allowed to make their homes all around the sacred mother mound. They soon received the gift of corn and learned to cultivate it in abundance, attaining a level of civilization to match the splendor of the agricultural paradise of the lower valley of the great river of the North American continent.

Intermediate Choctology

▼ ▼ ▼ ▼ ▼ ▼ ▼ ▼ ▼ ▼ ▼ ▼ ▼ ▼ ▼ ▼ ▼

When the Choctaws talk from the top of Rich Mountain, you have to go all the way to the panhandle to find anywhere in Oklahoma where anyone can do any taller talking. Rich Mountain is 2,660 feet high, whereas parts of the panhandle, and all the rest of Oklahoma, lie below 2,660 feet.

Once, the 4,438 feet northwestern corner boys tried to take the floor, figuring they had plenty enough feet over the Choctaws to have a taller talk. But the 4,973 foot obstruction of Black Mesa caused them to be poorly heard, and that, and the south wind blowing in favor of the Choctaws, caused the Choctaw talk to be more clearly heard over more of Oklahoma during the whole of the time that the 4,438 feet northwestern corner boys tried to hold the floor.

Once, the 1,558 feet southwestern corner boys tried to take the floor. But they came up 1,102 feet short.

Once, the 305 feet southeastern corner boys claimed that they had borrowed 2,356 feet from Black Mesa, and with that claim competed for the floor, claiming that Black Mesa had been reduced to 2,617 feet, thereby unobstructing much of the talk of the 4,438 feet northwestern corner boys, which was now giving the Choctaw talk enough competition from the northwestern corner to give the southeastern corner boys a say. But the northwestern corner boys continued to be poorly heard, and the south wind continued to blow in favor of the Choctaws, and the southeastern corner boys came up 2,355 feet short.

When the Choctaws talk from the 2,660 foot top of Rich Mountain, you have to go all the way to the panhandle to find anywhere in Oklahoma where anyone can do any taller talking.

Part I

▼ ▼ ▼ ▼ ▼ ▼ ▼ ▼ ▼

The Oklahoma
Basic Intelligence Test
Are You Smart Enough To Be An Okie?

▼ ▼ ▼ ▼ ▼ ▼ ▼ ▼ ▼ ▼ ▼ ▼ ▼ ▼ ▼

Instructions: Pretend you are an Okie. Mark as many answers to each question as you think might be correct (answers: pp. 17–18).

(1) "Okie" has been a derogatory term in California ever since the Dust Bowl days:

    A. because they found out about us when so many of us moved there

    B. because so many Californians actually got to know so many Okies

    C. due to personal observation by many Californians of Okie ways

    D. because so many Okies moved to California they could see how all of us must be

    E. because we could hardly claim to be any different than the many thousands of examples they could observe

(2) Some portion of what is today Oklahoma might have been visited in the 16th century by some members of the expeditions of which Spanish explorers?

    A. Coronado
    B. De Soto
    C. Camaro
    D. Toronado
    E. El Camino

(3) The wildlife refuge where the North Canadian River enters Lake Overholser in Oklahoma City is named:

   A. the Stenchcomb
   B. the Skunkcomb
   C. the Stinkcomb
   D. the Sludgecomb
   E. the Styrofoam Cupcomb

(4) Lake Overholser water is:

   A. safe to drink
   B. safe to walk on
   C. visible to astronauts at night
   D. Kodak's secret ingredient for developing color film
   E. sold as cattle dip in Texas

(5) Bird McGuire, Elmer Fulton, James Davenport, Charles Carter, and Scott Ferris were:

   A. the "Altus Five" defendants in a 1967 draft card burning case
   B. vice presidents of the United States
   C. Oklahoma's first congressmen
   D. head football coaches at Oklahoma University before World War II
   E. head football coaches at Oklahoma State University since World War II

(6) Oklahoma:
   A. is larger than any state east of it except Minnesota
   B. is smaller than any state north, south, or west of it except Washington and Hawaii
   C. is larger than the dark side of the moon, but smaller than the bright side of the moon
   D. is larger than all six New England states combined
   E. is fifty-seven times larger than Rhode Island

(7) Oklahoma:

    A. now has a higher ratio of water to land than Minnesota
    B. has one lake for every 2.3 registered voters
    C. has five governmental authorities authorized to develop, operate, and expand port facilities
    D. is approximately 305 feet above sea level at its lowest elevation and approximately 200 miles from the nearest ocean
    E. has one lake with a shoreline length roughly the equivalent of the round trip distance from Oklahoma City to Denver

(8) A person who aspires to be Governor of Oklahoma:

    A. wants to semi retire
    B. is a person of small ambition
    C. has not read the Oklahoma Constitution and does not know that he/she will have no power
    D. knows more contractors than you can find in the Yellow Pages
    E. couldn't get on at General Motors

(9) Ad Valorum taxes are:

    A. New Jersey-born radio sportscaster Al Eschback telling you the city and state where the new Sooner football recruit went to high school
    B. A tariff on Italian shoes
    C. a tax on Latin textbooks
    D. a soak the rich penalty for having more than one valet
    E. something the legislature did not want us to know about

(10) The historic Turner Turnpike:

    A. will be toll free once the construction cost has been collected

B. was where it all got started
C. had a TV show named after it
D. does not have a speed limit
E. is not open on Sundays, holidays, after 6:30 P.M. or before 5:30 A.M., and runs two to four times slower on Saturdays

(11) Oklahoma:

A. has a poison-berried parasite for a state floral emblem
B. pays several state employees a higher salary than the governor, because they have more important jobs
C. shares the infamous "tornado alley" with south-central Kansas
D. has the Ouachita Mountains, the Arbuckle Mountains, the Wichita Mountains, the Glass Mountains, the Kiamichi Mountains, the Winding Stair Mountains, the Boston Mountains, and the San Bois Mountains, but has no mountains
E. once dispatched troops against Texas in a dispute over a toll bridge.

(12) In Oklahoma:

A. the highest elevation is near the western end of the Panhandle, and the lowest elevation is near the SE corner of the state
B. the western end of the Panhandle is an extension of the High Plains of New Mexico and Colorado and contains antelope, while the SE corner of the state is an extension of the Gulf Coastal Plain and contains alligators
C. during one week snow drifts near Boise City in the Panhandle were six to nine feet deep, while at the same time the temperature near Idabel in the SE was 70 degrees
D. one year a county in the NW had a total annual rainfall of 6.63 inches, and the next year a reporting station in the SE had a total of 84.47 inches (and twelve years earlier had recorded 119 inches)

E. occasional sightings of Bigfoot occur in the SE, while in the NW there are occasional sightings of people

(13) Will Rogers was:

A. Governor of Oklahoma before he moved to Hollywood
B. Governor of Oklahoma after he lived in Hollywood
C. the first Oklahoma governor to die while in office
D. Oklahoma's first two-term governor
E. the only Oklahoma governor to be re-elected without opposition

(14) Football:

A. At the Ada High School football stadium the home town seats straddle the fifty yard line and are directly behind the team bench on the west side of the stadium
B. At the Ada High School football stadium the visitor's seats are on the east side of the stadium and extend only from the five yard line to the thirty-five yard line at the north end of the field
C. At the Ada High School football stadium the visitor's seats are set back about thirty yards from the field of play
D. At the Ada High School football stadium the visitor's seats face squarely into the blinding glare of the setting sun
E. Ada High School has won more state championships in football than any other Oklahoma high school

(15) If your mother says "drekly" when she means after awhile, says "cain't" instead of can't, and is always "fixin'" to do something:

A. you didn't go to OU because her threats to "put you in Norman" always sounded ominous
B. you still can't figure out why all the other guys complained about Army chow

   C. you know someone who knows someone who knew
      Cousin Minnie Pearl, and she wasn't really that way
      at all
   D. it was a cousin who first told you that motels do not
      bed down their guests on pallets on the floor
   E. if you could trade places with anyone in the world it
      would be with someone else in Oklahoma

(16) Old Greer County:

   A. was claimed by Texas, but was awarded to Indian
      Territory by the United States Supreme Court in a de-
      cision in March, 1896, and became a part of the State
      of Oklahoma in 1907
   B. was claimed by Oklahoma, but was awarded to Texas
      by the editors of *Sports Afield* on a map in the Au-
      gust, 1991 issue
   C. was where Darryl Royal came from
   D. is carved up into four SW Oklahoma counties
   E. cannot be gotten to by accident

(17) How did the expression "OK" enter the English language?

   A. President Andrew Jackson used it to initial his ap-
      proval of memos from his staff, an abbreviation for
      his spelling of "all correct"
   B. French port authorities are responsible for it, from
      the shipboard inspection of furs being imported from
      North America, from the phrase "c'est tres bien, en-
      voyez le au quai" (this is fine, send it to the dock),
      later shortened to "au quai"
   C. Californians began using it as a facetious non se-
      quitur after seeing so many license plates saying "Ok-
      lahoma is OK"
   D. High ranking American government officials picked
      it up from hearing Pushmataha's usage of the
      Choctaw word "hoke" to signify agreement or ap-
      proval
   E. Dime novelists picked it up from frequent interviews

with Wyatt Earp, who had begun using it to characterize a satisfactory outcome in a gunfight

(18) What is the best way to get some peace and quiet from relatives and in-laws in Oklahoma?

    A. drill a dry hole
    B. file for political office
    C. moonlight selling insurance
    D. get your own evangelical Christian television show
    E. begin a study of your family's genealogy

(19) It must be true:

    A. All watermelons for sale in Oklahoma were grown in Rush Springs
    B. 716,982 people attended the 1971 OU-Nebraska football game
    C. Oklahoma City has more furniture stores per capita than any place on earth
    D. The sports coverage of the *Daily Oklahoman* was half as extensive before the *Oklahoma City Times* folded and the *Daily Oklahoman* doubled its sports coverage
    E. God hates mobile homes

(20) We are not worried about the national debt because:

    A. It's all owed to the Japanese and the Arabs, and who are they gonna call?
    B. I didn't spend any of it
    C. I didn't borrow any of it
    D. It's all just on paper
    E. It's like an Indian treaty, isn't it?

Answers

  1. Any way you look at it, they've got the goods on us.
  2. They were all Spaniards, weren't they?

3. A is what the Okies named it.
4. Okies believe A to be correct.
5. You would skip this one (they were congressmen).
6. You would go outside at night and look before answering this one; all the others are true.
7. Because Okies hate running water, unless it comes out of a tap, you would mark B, hoping it will soon be correct, as the others are; the port authorities regulate barge traffic on the lakes where our rivers used to be; the lake in E is Grand Lake O' The Cherokees (it flooded their land and strangled their river, so the Okies named it after them in case they might want to take up water skiing they can feel at home).
8. Shame on you.
9. A lot of Sooner football players come from there.
10. If you marked A, send for free brochure "How to Invest in Staten Island Gold and Silver Mines"; if you marked C, you have this confused with "Route 66"; if you marked E, you have this confused with the Oklahoma City bus system.
11. It's quite a place.
12. Your cousin saw one crossing the highway once, but it was at night.
13. Will Rogers never became that kind of a comedian.
14. You can tell when the Chickasaws have had a hand in a thing; the Chickasaw Nation tribal headquarters is in Ada.
15. Yes, the state looney bin is also located in Norman.
16. Yes, a Sooner All America quarterback did become head coach at the University of Texas, but it just doesn't seem right.
17. Nobody knows.
18. All are proven methods.
19. It must be.
20. Treaties?

Have You Heard About America?

First they want to be your friends[1]

Then they want to build a wagon road
through where you live[2]

Then they want you to move[3]

Then they want to build a railroad
through where they moved you to[4]

Then they want to move in with you[5]

Then they want you to keep quiet
and stay out of their way
while they tell the world
that ever since then
your nation has been past tense

▼

---

[1]Treaty With The Choctaw, 1786
[2]Treaty With The Choctaw, 1801
[3]Treaty With The Choctaw, 1830
[4]Treaty With The Choctaw And Chickasaw, 1866
[5]Oklahoma Statehood, 1907

19

Using and
Misusing History
▼ ▼ ▼ ▼ ▼ ▼ ▼ ▼ ▼ ▼ ▼ ▼ ▼ ▼ ▼ ▼

You can tell an old timer by the way he talks. Take Bob
Giago, for example. To Giago, the Oklahoma City Indian
Clinic will, likely, forever be "the health project."

That's what it was at the beginning, and Giago was
there at the beginning. He is the only director the Oklahoma City office of the American Indian Training and Employment Program has ever had.

He's seen a lot, and it's reflected in his speech. He was
there when elements of the Oklahoma City Indian community pulled together to create and incorporate a Native
American Center, with which his program shared office
space, as did other Indian programs. They saw the desper-
ate need for an urban Indian health project, and in time
one came into being, at first consisting of medical students
volunteering their time to see patients at the Native American Center in the evenings. The health project blossomed,
incorporated in its own right, with its own funding and its
own board of directors, eventually moved out of the Native
American Center, as did most of the others, and went its
own way, known today as the Oklahoma City Indian
Clinic.

But to Giago, it's still "the health project."

If you are a novelist and you should have occasion in a
manuscript to have an Indian woman seek prenatal care at
that clinic, the history of the place is something your
reader probably does not need to know. But if you know it,
and you reveal a bit of it, perhaps by employing a character
patterned after an old timer like a Bob Giago, you will es-

tablish instant credibility with your reader to be writing about such things. You might never need to present your credentials again if you plant it in the mind of your reader early that you know what you are writing about.

A classic example of this technique is from a work of history. Legions of students have surveyed the Renaissance and the Reformation by way of the pithy prose of Henry Lucas. It's a big subject, almost more than one author could know. Yet, after working one's way through the fifth paragraph of his first chapter, which traces the claims of various parties to the crown of Naples, and in some cases also traces the ancestral lineage of claimants, a paragraph which must be diagrammed to be comprehended, and even then it's even money, few people have had it occur to them to question the author's credentials for attempting a nearly encyclopedic survey of that era.

Lucas never repeats such a passage, nor does he need to. The war to win the confidence of his reader is over. It was a short battle. It took place in the subconscious portion of the mind of the reader. And Lucas won it.

If you chose your opening to hit upon a strong point in your research you can do what Lucas did, though you'll undoubtedly not want to stop the flow of your story to do it.

Maybe a character patterned after an old timer like a Bob Giago could make a difference in an opening scene, someone who reveals by the way he talks that he didn't just fall off the turnip truck. A quiet analysis of how his speech differs from others could be a vehicle for slipping in enough concrete, specific details from your research to lull the reader into accepting everything else you say at face value.

But while you might capitalize on the anomaly of an old timer referring to the present in terms of the past, you must guard against referring to the past in terms of the present.

Let's look at a completely harmless example first. In a magazine article an author says "A British-American standoff persisted in northern California until the 1845 war with Mexico resulted in the annexation of most of the Southwest, including all of California." *problem*

The problem here is that the United States did not annex all of California. Alta California, yes; Baja California, no. All of California? No way. You might say, "But Baja California is in Mexico." But isn't that the point? So was Alta California.

Trivial? Yes. The author's use of the term "northern" conjures up images of the way the present state of California is divided between a northern and southern section for many kinds of references, and his "most of the southwest" lends further support to a conclusion that he has in mind the contemporary borders of that region (except for the Gadsden Purchase). Undoubtedly the author means "the present state of California."

But that isn't what he says, and he uses the term in such a way that the more one knows about the long history of Spain in America, and the Mexican War, and the negotiations for the treaty of Guadalupe Hidalgo for what would remain Mexican and what would become American, the more careless the remark will seem.

If you set your novel in that region in that era it will be just such readers your book likely will attract.

In this instance the carelessness of the remark about California turned out to be merely a preface to an error of fact that followed in the very next sentence, where the author missed the date of the promulgation of the Monroe Doctrine by seventeen years. Since much of the remainder of the article concerned difficult-to-verify information about the fur trade, how much confidence would you place in that information?

I believe this author got himself in trouble by the unhistorical mindset which he brought to writing history. If the remainder of the article had been outstanding then his lapse of referring to the past in terms of the present might have been overlooked. But, as is so often the case, it turned out to be a warning to a wary reader that this author was in trouble.

The quickest way I know to get into trouble in this regard is in writing about Indians. The problem here is that so much of what has been published that you might want to rely upon in your research, even reference books, especially reference books, has been written so as to distort history, and one of the most common vehicles in that attempt has been to refer to the past in terms of the present.

Suppose you were to decide to set your novel among Indians. Suppose you were to choose one of the so-called Five Civilized Tribes, the Choctaw Indians.

You begin your research by consulting reference books. See if you can spot any problem with this statement from the *American Indian Almanac*, in an otherwise excellent entry about the Choctaws: "After being forced to cede their lands in Mississippi and Alabama and to move to Oklahoma, the Choctaw established their own government."

The problem here is that while Mississippi and Alabama were in existence at the time of Choctaw removal (early 1830s), Oklahoma was not. "Oklahoma" has no geographical significance except as a reference to constitutionally created entities (a territory in 1890; a state in 1907). Therefore, in the early 1830s the Choctaws could not have been moved there.

Oklahoma is a term meaning "Red People," consisting of the Choctaw words *okla* (people) and *humma* (red). Because the Choctaw word *humma* has come to be spelled "homa" in the name "Oklahoma," one frequently sees the name translated as "Home of the Red Man," but "home" is no part of the term; Choctaw words for home are *aiilli*, *chuka*, and *yakni*.

The term was suggested by Choctaw Principal Chief Allen Wright as a designation for the new territory being created in what was roughly the western half of the present state. "Oklahoma" becomes a term of geographical reference only very near that date (1890).

Now that we've got the hang of it, let's see if the *Colum-*

bia-Viking Desk Encyclopedia can do any better. Can you spot the problem in its entry for "Choctaw Indians," where, in its cryptic style we find: "Were removed to the Indian Territory in 1832."

The problem here, as the "Indian Territory" entry in the same encyclopedia will tell you, is that Indian Territory did not come into existence until the Indian Intercourse Act of 1834.

So where were the Choctaws removed to? Where, indeed. And why all the fuss, anyway? Isn't this just splitting hairs, technicalities, all just . . . history, all very similar to the trivial example about California?

No, it is not, and the reasons will present themselves shortly. To help get there, let's look at another reference book.

Consider this entry for "Choctaw Indians" from the *Basic Everyday Encyclopedia*: "After the Revolution settlers poured into the Gulf area and, in 1831–32, the C moved to a reservation on the Red R in SE Oklahoma, where they set up a US-style government."

Sounds like they just decided to pick up and go, doesn't it? And it sounds like there was already a place called Oklahoma and that the good people of that place made room for the Choctaws by letting them have a reservation in the southeastern part of it.

This kind of history stands history on its head. Such an entry is called advocacy journalism. It has a point of view, in this case to pretty up two events, one of which was one of the most inhumane, genocidal, and mean-spirited episodes in American history, the forced march of the Choctaws, from their ancestral homeland east of the Mississippi River, ill-provisioned and in the dead of winter, and the other is to cover up the betrayal of the Choctaws by the United States after their removal.

If you have any interest in, or stomach for, the details of the removal, historians have uncovered them in sickening abundance, and I commend their work, in university libraries, to you.

But back to the *Basic Everyday Encyclopedia*. Note the term "reservation." What might this be?

Listen to the language of Article IV of "Treaty with the Choctaw, 1830," commonly referred to as the Choctaw removal treaty or the treaty of Dancing Rabbit Creek, from Charles J. Kappler's *Laws and Treaties*, Vol. II: "The Government and people of the United States are hereby obligated to secure to the said Choctaw Nation of Red People the jurisdiction and government of all the persons and property that may be within their limits west, so that no territory or state shall ever have a right to pass laws for the government of the Choctaw Nation of Red People and their descendants; and that no part of the land granted them shall ever be embraced in any territory or state; . . . "

Ouch. Now we know why special pleaders and apologists and other practitioners of advocacy journalism have been in such a hurry to get the Choctaws into "Oklahoma" or "Indian Territory," so as to avoid mentioning where the Choctaws were, in fact, removed to, namely, their own sovereign nation, with guarantees of that sovereignty.

What might appear as mere technicalities and hair splitting regarding these examples of referring to the past in terms of the present now emerge as something more than just history. It has relevance (where public opinion cannot easily be ignored) in titanic legal battles regarding contemporary issues of Indian sovereignty that occupy the time of such people as justices of the United States Supreme Court.

What you write and how you write it will have an influence on all who read it. You may not want to deal with controversial, emotionally charged political disputes in your novel, but if you write, innocently, that the Choctaws were removed to "Oklahoma" or to "Indian Territory" you unwittingly align yourself on one side of the dispute, and you perpetuate myth or disinformation or whatever you want to call it.

If you want to align yourself on one side or the other, that is your right, but get your facts right. If you're going to write about Indians, take the time to read their treaties before you begin to write.

Just because there's a dispute taking place doesn't mean you have to be frightened away from any region or any era or any subject. You can avoid many potential problems when you set your historical novel in a place now called Oklahoma if you are aware that much of what has been published about Indians and about Oklahoma, especially for consumption by the general public or for secondary schools, has been written in such a way as to distort unpleasant events which speak volumes about the American national character, then and now (Oklahoma's Indians, overwhelmed and ignored, trying desperately to save their cultures from extinction, are still there, still pointing to the treaties, still waiting).

Awareness of the problem is your most important safeguard as you do your research. In addition to reading the treaties, you can gain this awareness in no better way than by reading *And Still The Waters Run* by Angie Debo (Princeton University Press, 1940).

Once you've gained awareness you can laugh, or cry, or get angry right along with the Indians as you read much of what has been published about them.

And for your own book, if you open by hitting upon a strong point in your research, gain the confidence of your reader, and then concentrate on the story you have to tell, you can have confidence that while you may not be writing history you'll not be distorting it, either.

Anna Lewis:
Choctaw Historian

▼ ▼ ▼ ▼ ▼ ▼ ▼ ▼ ▼ ▼ ▼ ▼ ▼ ▼ ▼ ▼

Anna Lewis was born in the Choctaw Nation in 1885, near the beginning of the fifth century of the holocaust. By the time of her birth the dispossession of the North American continent was far advanced. She grew to maturity listening to American justifications for the genocidal assault on Native culture, Native language, Native religion, and Native political sovereignty. Her own people, the Choctaws, were in the midst of being dispossessed of their republic by the Dawes Commission, a process that would culminate in the unlawful creation of the state of Oklahoma in 1907.

The betrayal of the Choctaw people by the United States was so blatant that Choctaws could only react with stunned disbelief. Throughout the nineteenth century Choctaws had relied upon the explicit provisions of article four of *Treaty With The Choctaw, 1830*, which guarantees their sovereignty, and that their nation shall never be a part of any territory or state. It was this treaty by which the Choctaws had been forced to abandon their ancestral homelands east of the Mississippi River and had been removed to their new land west of the Mississippi, in three, successive, brutal winter migrations that killed 2,500 of them.

As she watched her nation being illegally dismantled, Anna Lewis determined to do something about it. She could not save her country, but she could make certain that Choctaws of future generations would know the truth of what had been done to them, and that they would know the injustice of it. She dedicated her life to the study, teaching, and writing of Choctaw history.

Her academic career was distinguished by many accomplishments. Among them, she became, in 1930, the first woman to receive the Doctor of Philosophy degree from the University of Oklahoma. Having begun her schooling at the Tushkahoma Female Institute in the Choctaw Nation, she had also earned the A.B. and M.A degrees from the University of California at Berkeley. The great majority of her professional life, until her retirement in 1956, was spent as head of the department of history at the Oklahoma College for Women in Chickasha, Oklahoma.

Her doctoral dissertation was published as a book in 1932 under the title *Along The Arkansas* (Southwest Press), which is a study of French-Indian relations along the lower Arkansas River valley in the eighteenth century. Throughout her life she contributed many articles to scholarly journals.

Her life's work, however, a labor of twenty years, is a definitive biography of the great Okla Hannali Choctaw war chief, Pushmataha. Research for this manuscript was conducted at libraries at the University of California, the University of Oklahoma, the State Library of Mississippi, and the Library of Congress.

Why she was unable to find a publisher for this book will remain one of the great injustices in the history of American publishing. Why she was unable to find a publisher, however, is not much of a mystery.

Anna Lewis completed her biography of Pushmataha in the 1950s during one of the most intellectually repressive eras in American history. Official government policy on the part of the United States was one of "termination" of Indian nations. Locked in a nuclear "cold war" with the Soviet Union, Americans viewed as treason any criticism of themselves or their past. What Anna Lewis had to say about American history and the American national character was criticism of the harshest kind, documented truth.

In 1960, perhaps because she realized that she was in failing health and would not have long to continue trying to find a publisher (she died in 1961), Anna Lewis, to the undying gratitude of all future generations of Choctaws, with the help of money borrowed from her sister, paid to have the book published by a vanity press in New York City.

Chief Pushmataha—American Patriot: The Story of the Choctaws' Struggle for Survival (New York: Exposition Press, 1960) is, despite its title, anything but a work of American patriotism. It is a straightforward account of the injustice of the betrayal of the Choctaw people by the United States.

The message of the book is carried by a simple recitation of the career of Pushmataha, showing the indebtedness of the United States to the Choctaws, who, under Pushmataha's leadership, sided with the United States on the great issue of the day, whether or not to join Tecumseh's pan-Indian confederation against the Americans during the War of 1812.

Pushmataha faced Tecumseh in open debate in front of the assembled Choctaw leaders and warriors in the fall of 1811 on Tecumseh's visit to the southern nations. As a result of Pushmataha's vigorous opposition to Tecumseh, Tecumseh was expelled from the Choctaw country. In the ensuing War of 1812, Pushmataha led Choctaw troops, which at times numbered as many as 800, in decisive battles against the Tecumseh faction of the Creeks (who were known as Red Sticks) and against the British at the Battle of New Orleans, operating as Choctaw auxiliaries for General Andrew Jackson's U.S. Army.

The Choctaws had won the friendship and allegiance of the United States, not by the grace and generosity of the United States, but by virtue of Choctaw blood shed on the battlefields on behalf of the United States. Under Pushmataha's leadership the Choctaw Nation cast its lot with the Americans, only to be betrayed within less than twenty years by their forced removal to the West, and by the eventual extinction of the new Choctaw republic in the West shortly after the end of the century.

Among the book's original contributions to knowledge, Anna Lewis discovered, in candid, but long-neglected, State Department reports, that Andrew Jackson had secured the signature of Okla Falaya Choctaw war chief Puckshennubbe to the treaty of 1820 by means of blackmail. Puckshennubbee's daughter had married an American soldier, who had deserted; Jackson learned of this and threatened to have Puchshennubbe's son-in-law executed if the chief did not sign the treaty.

There are many other noteworthy things about the book. Of particular significance, Anna Lewis was among the first to make extensive use of the eye-witness accounts of frontier physician and naturalist Dr. Gideon Lincecum, who had operated a store on the fringes of the Choctaw country in Mississippi, had learned fluent Choctaw, and who had observed some of the more dramatic events in the Choctaw country in the decade before removal. Lincecum, who later moved to Texas and published a study of fire ants in London, a paper which was sponsored by Charles Darwain, was an opponent of Christian missionaries in the Choctaw country. Lincecum had a reverence for Choctaw traditional life. He collected and recorded Choctaw traditional stories, as well as examples of the medicinal properties of plants used by Choctaw physicians, and he wrote a grammar of the Choctaw language, as well as a biography of Pushmataha, who he knew personally. Many of Lincecum's papers were water damaged and destroyed during the American War Between the States, but his biography of Pushmataha, along with his own autobiography (reconstructed from letters to a grandson), were published posthumously in the early twentieth century by the Mississippi Historical Society.

Among Lincecum's observations was one that gives a hint of the sanctity of freedom of speech in Choctaw traditional life and which shows how little indebted Choctaws are to the United States for cherished fundamental liberties. Lincecum tells of the manner in which the Choctaws debated the public issues of the day. A large brush arbor was constructed, one with a hole in the center of the roof. Whoever might desire to speak was required to stand beneath the hole, in the full heat of the Mississippi sun, while the audience remained comfortably seated in the shade. The Choctaws told Lincecum they could bear to sit and listen as long as the speaker could bear to stand and speak.

Imbued with this sort of knowledge about the ancient practices of her people and an intimate acquaintance with the characteristics of her people as she had known them in her lifetime, Anna Lewis wrote a book that Choctaws can turn to for the truth about their past. She suffered for her candidness, for her single-minded devotion to telling the Choctaw story. She did not have the satisfaction of seeing her book published by a respected university press. That did not stop her from finding a way to get it published, and for that she is deeply revered by her people.

For additional information:

"Anna Lewis, A Great Woman of Oklahoma," by Winnie Lewis Gravitt, in *The Chronicles of Oklahoma*, Winter, 1962–63, Volume XL, Number 4, pps. 326–329.

Chief Pushmataha: American Patriot, The Story of the Choctaws' Struggle for Survival, by Anna Lewis. New York: Exposition Press, 1960.

"Contributions By Choctaw Women To The Study Of Choctaw History," by D.L. Birchfield, in "Celebrating the Circle: Recognizing Women and Children in Restoring the Balance." *Gatherings: The En'owkin Journal of First North American Peoples*, Volume V, Fall 1994. Penticton, British Columbia, Canada: Theytus Books, Ltd., pps. 47–51.

History of the Choctaw, Chickasaw, and Natchez Indians, by H.B. Cushman; edited, with a foreword by Angie Debo. Stillwater, OK: Redlands Press, 1962 (originally published, 1899).

"Life of Apushimataha," by Gideon Lincecum, in *Publications of the Mississippi Historical Society*, Volume 9, 1905–1906, pps. 415–485.

The Rise and Fall of the Choctaw Republic, by Angie Debo. Norman: University of Oklahoma Press, 1934, 2nd edition, 1961.

Point of Purchase

▼ ▼ ▼ ▼ ▼ ▼ ▼ ▼ ▼ ▼ ▼ ▼ ▼ ▼ ▼ ▼

In the middle of the University of Oklahoma Book Exchange Joel started to vanish. As he walked up and down the aisles, from one side of the bookstore to the other, less and less of him was visible until, finally, he completely disappeared behind a double armful of used textbooks, which is a good trick for a Chickasaw who stands six foot four and weighs two hundred and eighty pounds.

"Christ," he said, "six books for one class, eight for another. They think I'm made out of money?"

"You're rich," I said. And he was; Pell grant, Otag grant, student loan, the somebody-something-or-other essay writing award, money from his summer job, his mother's money.

"Anything else I need?" he said, standing sideways to be able to see me.

"A dictionary."

"Jesus, I've got a dictionary. I've got three dictionaries."

"Yeah, but there's one here on sale." We stood in front of the checkout counter, looking at a stack of cellophane-wrapped, hardback, desk-size dictionaries. One of them was unwrapped, standing open on a book holder.

"They're Webster's," he said. "You hate Webster's. Let's go."

"Wait a minute," I said. "I want to give it the acid test."

I flipped through the pages, stopping at "hypolimnion." As I read the entry I knew immediately that I had to have this dictionary. Finally a lexicographer had gotten around to reading *Lucas On Bass Fishing*, by Jason Lucas.

As fishing columnist for *Sports Afield*, the old *Sports Afield*, before it went yuppie, Lucas had been one of the first to explain why you can't catch fish in the summertime in deep water that doesn't have any oxygen in it.

There wasn't any deep water around here until the _# 7_ Okies got here, until they decided we didn't need a place of our own and took over. It was all stream fishing. But Okies hate running water. Why, I don't know. But they do. If a valley narrows just a little bit they call it a dam site and you wake up one morning and find a lake where the river used to be. They're building a new one, or planning a new one, every waking moment. And It's been going on for decades. According to the *Historical Atlas of Oklahoma*, Oklahoma now has a higher ratio of water to land than Minnesota. Around here it's either learn to fish in a lake or learn to quit fishing.

> Learn to like wind, learn to like spray
> Yearn to be on a lake every day
>
> There ain't no lake right here yet
> But give the Okies a few more years
> And there'll be a lake here yet
>
> Learn to like wind, learn to like spray
> Yearn to be on a lake every day
>
> There ain't no lake right there yet
> But give the Okies a few more years
> And there'll be a lake there yet
>
> Learn to like wind, learn to like spray
> Yearn to be on a lake every day
>
> There ain't no lake over yonder yet
> But give the Okies a few more years
> And there'll be a lake over yonder yet

I looked up at Joel. "It's got hypolimnion. If it's got hypolimnion, it'll have epilimnion and thermocline too"

"Big deal," said Joel. "I don't need another dictionary."

I picked up one of the cellophane-wrapped volumes and wedged it between his chin and the top of one of the stacks he was holding. His eyes narrowed to a pig-like stare. He stood there, not saying anything.

"Put it back," I said, "If you can."

It made a fine capstone, I thought, sitting atop a volume of 18th century English poetry, a second-year German grammar review, an elementary Latin text, and several 18th century English novels.

Finally, he said, "How much is it?"

"Ten ninety-five. Marked down from eighteen ninety-five."

"It was published sometime this century?"

I examined the display copy. "Nineteen eighty-eight."

He accepted defeat with a "humph" and pushed past me to the checkout stand. But when the clerk rang up the $10.95 for the dictionary he gave me that same narrow-eyed, pig-like stare. He said, "At least it's a hardback."

As we walked across campus I thumbed through my only purchase, a paperback, the press guide for the 1990 Sooner varsity football team.

"You see," said Joel, pointing at my press guide, "you buy the paperback edition rather than the hardback."

"It doesn't come in hardback."

"Doesn't matter," he said. "If it only came in hardback you wouldn't own it. You wouldn't own it because you wouldn't buy it. You wouldn't buy it because you're too cheap to shell out the price of a hardback."

He was right so I kept my mouth shut, which is an awkward moment in the mentor/protege relationship, and one generally to be avoided wherever possible. I could see right there that it was going to be a delicate matter separating him from his new dictionary.

▼

I had talked him into taking a short trip, so we crossed the Canadian River and entered the Chickasaw Nation, driving southeast until we came to the town of Ada, where the Chickasaw Nation tribal headquarters are located. Across town, we found ourselves seated in the Ada high school football stadium.

We were sitting on the visitor's side, nestled between the dozens of moms and dads and grandfathers and grandmothers of the Moore Lions high school football team, who, like us, had made the hour and a half drive from the Oklahoma City area to watch a pre-season, controlled scrimmage.

You can tell when the Chickasaws have had a hand in a thing, the Ada High School football stadium being a case in point. The visitor's seats are set back from the field of play about thirty yards. What's worse, they extend only from the goal line to the thirty-five yard line at the north end of the field. And they face squarely into the blinding glare of the setting sun.

Across the way, the Ada Cougar hometown seats straddle the fifty yard line and are set directly behind the team bench at the very edge of the field. It wouldn't take much imagination to picture the differences between the locker room facilities.

You have to admire a program like Ada. Fourteen state championships in football, more than any other Oklahoma high school, attest to the thoroughness and thoughtfulness of every other detail. With predictable regularity, every three or four years, they produce at least one outstanding college player, who almost always becomes a Sooner. And that's why we were here, to get a peek at the future, an obligation of being a conscientious Sooner fan. For me it was also an obligation of being a mentor to a promising young fellow who showed disturbing signs of having difficulty getting his priorities straight.

"They've got a kid at quarterback," I explained to Joel,

"a left-handed quarterback who just might be one of the finest pure athletes in this region of the country. He's only going to be a junior this year. And the Moore quarterback is one of the fastest kids in the state."

"Big deal," said Joel. "Drive all this way to watch a scrimmage. No band, no cheerleaders, not even any pom pon girls."

"And no admission charge either. Relax. You can't spend your whole life sitting on your butt reading books."

"I could be reading one now," said Joel, sourly surveying his surroundings. He was squinting his eyes, trying to see into the glare of the sun. "How are we supposed to be able to see the field?"

The two teams put on quite a show, especially when the quarterback from Moore set sail on a seventy yard touchdown scramble that left every Cougar on the field trying to tackle where he had just been. That set the crowd to buzzing. It was worth the three-hour, round-trip drive, and no charge for admission.

At least I thought so, but Joel was restless and bored the whole evening. Even moving over to the Ada side, where we could see, didn't help. I remembered a time, not so long ago, when he had played tackle on a visiting team in that very stadium. But even then he'd rather have been reading a book, like as not one of those old novels, the kind that are deadly boring because nothing ever happens in them. Except for that flaw in his character he might have played college ball.

Later, driving back, Joel was still bored. He tried to start several conversations, but staring into the sun had made me too tired to do anything but slump down in the seat and nap with my eyes half open.

Finally, he said, "Man, oh, man, if you're what it's like to be past forty, shoot me before I turn thirty."

"That's a deal," I said, half intending to do it.

▼

That night we were back in the city, at the coffee counter at Mama Lou's, our hangout. The nap had done wonders for me.

"It's got the f-word," I said.

Joel didn't stop reading, except to glance over at his new dictionary, laying open on the counter in front of me, and grin.

Twenty minutes later I said, "This is the most artful definition I've ever read."

Joel didn't look up. For two or three minutes he continued reading, until he came to a convenient breaking point. He picked up a little pink packet of Sweet 'N Low, placed it somewhere deep in the middle of *Ullyses*, and set the book aside. He said, "Oh, yeah, what?"

"'Choctaw,'" I said. "According to this the Choctaws are 'a North American Indian people.' That's a pretty sophisticated phrase."

He read the entry, then sat staring straight ahead thinking God knows what, waiting for me to go on. Being Chickasaw, but not being more than moderately interested in his heritage, he had grown accustomed to finding himself at the butt of clumsy jokes about how the Chickasaws really were only a branch of the Choctaws and would one day come back to the fold. But this time I was serious.

→ "This phrase catfoots across a whole minefield of potential problems," I said. "It avoids classifying the Choctaws as a tribe, which would imply that we are a dependent domestic minority rather than a sovereign nation. Likewise, it avoids using the word 'nation,' which would imply sovereignty and get the lexicographer in trouble with those who have a vested interest in denying that the Choctaws hold that status, such as officials of the state of Oklahoma and the federal government. It dodges that issue even further by using the geographical term 'North American,' rather than a political term like 'United States,' to give the location. It does use the word 'Indian,' which is beginning to come back into vogue, even though it's a laughable misnomer and a geographical absurdity. But it avoids the use of 'Native American,' which didn't appear in any dictionary until 1959, in a Scribner's. Do you think 'Native American' implies dependent domestic minority status?"

Joel was quiet for a moment, then said, "Why don't you just admit that the Choctaws, like every other Indian tribe, are a dependent domestic minority, and give history a chance to catch up with you?"

I could not believe what I was hearing. "Because we are a sovereign nation," I said. "In 1820 we traded five million acres of the richest farmland east of the Mississippi for eleven million acres west of the Mississippi, more than half of it arid plains. In 1825 they forced us to give up all of our western land that is now part of Arkansas. In 1830 we lost all of our western land that is now part of north-eastern New Mexico and the Texas panhandle and we gave up the rest of our land east of the Mississippi, millions of acres, and were forced to move to this God-forsaken place, and got nothing in exchange but a guarantee of sovereignty for our nation in what amounted to the southern half of what they think is now the state of Oklahoma."

I knew I could nail his butt simply by quoting from article four of the removal treaty, the Treaty of Dancing Rabbit Creek: "The Government and people of the United States are hereby obliged to secure to the said Choctaw Nation of Red People the jurisdiction and government of all the persons and property that may be within their limits west, so that no territory or state shall ever have a right to pass laws for the government of the Choctaw Nation of Red People and their descendants; and that no part of the land granted them shall ever be embraced in any territory or state, ..." But I wanted to be sure he understood how Pushmataha's military exploits on behalf of the United States had put the Choctaws in a position to secure for themselves the guarantees of article four, and that required going back about twenty years before the treaty, to about the time Tecumseh came south to meet Pushmataha in debate.

Like an evangelical Christian witnessing to some lost soul, I was poised to see if I could bring the heathen to salvation, when I saw he was grinning at me.

He said, "You gonna start with the removal treaty or you gonna go all the way back to Tecumseh and Pushmataha?"

"OK," I said, "I give up."

"You're sure?" said Joel. "I will listen to it again if you want to run through it. You know, see if you leave anything out. I'm worried you might be losing your touch. Last time you left out the tirade about how Americans don't even know anything about Pushmataha."

"Ok, Ok," I said. "It's hopeless."

He nodded, then reached for *Ullyses*.

Before he could bury himself in the book, I wanted to let him know that I wasn't the least bit offended by his attitude, which wasn't altogether the truth. I said, "You're supposed to be reading eighteenth century English novels."

"Huh uh," he said. "Not 'til next week. I'm still on break."

As casually as I could manage it, I said, "Tell you what. I feel kinda bad about you getting stuck with this dictionary. How about if I give you five dollars for it, and you can get some of your money back."

He said, "What? I just paid eleven bucks for it."

"Look," I said, "that was grant money you were throwing around, and you've still got a ton of it left to spend. Besides, it's now a used book. It depreciated at least fifty percent the minute you walked out of the bookstore with it. And you've got three other dictionaries. You said, yourself, you don't need this one."

He glanced longingly at *Ullyses*, then turned his full attention to me. "What you want is a hardback dictionary at a paperback price. No, let me rephrase that. You want *my* hardback dictionary at a paperback price."

"You said you didn't need it."

"Uh huh. You found something else in there you like, didn't you?"

"A few things."

"Like what?"

I opened the dictionary to "Aretino, Pietro." I said, "It has biographical entries. And this one is evidence of real scholarship."

Joel read the entry. He said, "All it says is: '1492–1556; Italian satirical writer.'"

"True. But it doesn't say, 'Illegitimate, wretchedly evil, Renaissance Italian, atheist pornographer who died from a blow to the head sustained while falling over backward in his chair in a fit of laughter upon hearing of some lewd act of one of his sisters.'"

"The false biography," said Joel.

"That's right," I said, remembering that Joel had read a paper I once wrote about Aretino, and that he had maneuvered me into admitting that the paper was poorly written.

"What was the deal with this guy?" said Joel, wrinkling his brow, but whether he was actually trying to remember or only pretending he couldn't remember, I couldn't tell.

"He was an extortionist," I said. "He was such an incredibly gifted satirical poet he made a fortune blackmailing the rich and powerful by promising not to make them the laughing stock of Europe in his lampoons. After he died they got even by concocting a false biography that held sway for centuries. Even the eleventh edition of the *Encyclopaedia Brittanica* swallowed it whole."

"He was blacklisted," said Joel.

"Postumously," I said. "The whole cultural memory of him was blacklisted. Either he just wasn't mentioned at all or some sketch of the false biography was given. It's only been in this century that—"

"You don't think it should say more than just Italian satirist?

"Like what?"

"Oh, that he might be the father of modern journalism?"

"I was getting to that."

Joel grinned. "I could tell."

"Look, the important point here is that you've got to be on your toes academically to be aware of changes in a person's reputation who died more than five hundred years ago. 'Italian satirical writer' may sound pretty sparse, but that's what he was, maybe the best that ever was, and that's why he should be remembered."

"And in my dictionary," said Joel, "he is remembered. You like my new dictionary, don't you?"

"It's OK."

"Let's see, it's got your buddy Aretino; you can read the Choctaw entry without giving yourself a stroke; you can use it as a springboard to rattle on about lake fishing to anyone who'll listen about epilimnions and hypolimnions and how to find the thermocline. Anything in there about football?"

I shrugged.

Joel looked at the clock. He began gathering up his things, including his dictionary. "Yes, sir, if it were a paperback that would just about make it perfect, wouldn't it? But it's not. It's a hardback. And it's mine. And it's time for my beddy bye."

▼

The next day I was rushing in and out of the supermarket, picking up a new notebook, and there, right in front of the "10 Items or Less, Cash Only" checkout counter, in a paperback rack, was Joel's dictionary, the paperback edition of Joel's dictionary.

There was only one of its kind on the rack. I snatched it up and retreated a few paces to examine it. It had to be the same dictionary. The covers were identical, white and yellow print on a red background. And on the cover was the final proof: "Based on 'The Best Desk Dictionary Available' the Third College Edition of Webster's New World Dictionary."

Rarely, maybe never, have I experienced such cheerful satisfaction at forking over $4.50, plus tax, for any book.

At the coffee shop Joel was unaware of my arrival until I plopped the paperback on top the page he was reading.

I gauged the effect by the fact he forgot to put a place marker in *Ullyses* as he set it aside.

"Where did you find this?" he said.

"At the supermarket."

"How much?"

"Four-fifty."

"Exactly the same as mine?"

"Nineteen ninety edition," I said.

"Let's compare." He hauled his dictionary out of his bookbag and handed it to me. He looked at the title page of my paperback. He said, "Victoria Neufeldt, Editor in Chief."

I looked at the title page of his hardback. "Victoria Neufeldt, Editor in Chief." I could not keep from gloating.

We each read further into the front matter, skipping around, ticking off points of comparison, until Joel read something in my paperback that stopped me cold.

"Order of senses," he said. "The standard, general senses of a word are given first, . . . "

"What?" I said. "That doesn't sound like a Webster's to me. That's why I don't like Webster's. You've got to wade through the etymology first, before you get to the definitions, then they're arranged according to the oldest, most archaic meanings of the word."

He showed me the page he had been reading.

I quickly located the corresponding page in the front matter of his hardback. I read out loud: "The senses have in general been arranged in historical order, from the etymology (usually the sense or senses of a word before modern English times or in the language or languages from which it came) through the original modern English senses (now often archaic or obsolete) to the most recent senses. Thus the most common present-day meaning of a word may appear near the end of an entry."

"See what I mean?" I said. "With your hardback it's like wading through molasses to get to the currently accepted meaning." I pointed to my paperback. "But that is something a person can actually use."

He looked chagrined, so I waded in. He endured about ten minutes of exposition while I lauded the virtues of lightweight, portable paperbacks compared to the ponderous thing he had purchased. He had to admit that I was right when I pointed out that, on those rare occasions when he had any interest at all in the precise historical evolution of a word, he could get a much more thorough, more exhaustively scholarly historical ordering of the senses from the *Oxford English Dictionary* or even the unabridged Webster's. I took pains to have him admit, to have him actually say it, that he hardly ever went to a dictionary, any dictionary, to trace the evolution of a word within the language. I had to be careful about etymology, because he had an interest in etymology, in how the word came to be a part of the English lexicon, and from what language it had originated, so I had to step lightly around etymology. But that wasn't difficult to do.

Finally, when I thought the time was right, I said, "Tell you what I'll do. I'll swap dictionaries with you. That's a pretty even deal, and you get a good, portable dictionary that you can actually use. It'll be a lot less weight in your bookbag. What do you say?"

What he said was, completely ignoring my offer, "I can't believe they'd go to all the trouble of rearranging the order of senses."

Here was my chance to close the deal. I said, "Let's check it out. Pick a word."

He thought for a moment. "How about 'fair?' That has a lot of different senses."

"That's a good one," I said.

He found it first, in the paperback. "One," he said, "attractive, beautiful."

"One," I said, "attractive, beautiful, lovely."

We looked at each other.

"What are the odds on that?" he said. "The oldest meaning is still the standard, general sense of the word?"

"Sure," I said. "Why not?"

"Two," he said, "unblemished, clean."

"Two," I said, "unblemished, clean."

He looked at me.

I shrugged. "It happens, I guess."

"Three," he said, "blond."

I cleared my throat.

"Un huh," he said.

"Well, It could happen, couldn't it?"

"Did it?"

"Well, yeah, it did."

"Sure it did. Do you have any idea what the statistical probability on that would be, on three in a row?"

"Let's try another word."

"Why?" he said, visibly warming to the one at hand. He read again, "Four, five, six . . . clear and sunny . . . easy to read . . . just and honest." He looked over at the hardback. "Four, five, six . . . clear and sunny . . . easy to read . . . just and honest." He looked up. "Need I go on?"

"Look," I said, "The eights are different."

But he wasn't having any of it. He picked up the paperback. He said, "I'll give it *my* acid test."

He flipped to the entry for Oklahoma. "Ah ha," he said, "69,919 square miles, but no square kilometers."

"Square kilometers?"

He reached over and tapped his fingers on his hardback. But before I could open it, he said, "Wait a minute. Where's the etymology?"

"No etymology?"

"None," he said. He reached over, picked up his hardback, flipped to "Oklahoma," and pointed, with smug satisfaction. "'Oklahoma,'" he said, "'from the Choctaw *okla*, people, plus *homma*, red.'" He handed me my paperback.

"OK," I said, after a few moments of staring at the entry, "so they left out the etymologies."

"Huh uh," he said. He'd been scanning the page I was

looking at. "There's one. There's another. There's another one. Abbreviated etymologies, but etymologies nonetheless." He looked up at me. "They only left out some of them. And one of them they left out was probably the only Choctaw word that might have made it into the dictionary in the first place. How does that grab you?"

It didn't grab me particularly well, but I recovered enough to flip to "Colorado" in the paperback, and, as I suspected, it had no etymology either. "So," I said, "they simply left out etymologies for the states in the paperback edition. They had to leave out something."

"Uh huh," he said. He'd been looking back and forth at both dictionaries. "Yours doesn't give the date admitted to statehood either."

I don't remember what I was about to say when he hit me with the big one. "Oh, you're going to love this. It doesn't even have 'Choctaw.'"

"What?"

He handed the paperback to me. I was so jolted, when I couldn't find the entry, that I couldn't find where it should have been, could not remember how to spell it. I had to look at the hardback, at the sequence of entries . . . 'chocolatier, Choctaw, choice . . . " before I was able to figure out that it should have fallen between chocolate and choice, in the paperback, but it was not there.

The rest of it was like a bad dream. In painful succession he discovered there was no entry for hypolimnion: "Gee, if it doesn't have hypolimnion, no use even looking for epilimnion and thermocline;" no entry for Pietro Aretino: "Guess the sucker is back on the blacklist;" and some really painful shots: "Hey, it's got 'Cherokee;'" and, "Hey, it's got 'Apache.' And listen to this, the Apaches are 'a group of SW U.S. Indians.' No waffling there on the old dependent domestic minority issue." He found a lot of things to compare, to comment on. "I guess when you drop from 170,000 entries to 59,600 you have to shake out the chaff."

I had long since surrendered when he finally said, "You know, by rights, it would be fitting if you just gave me this paperback dictionary."

"Here," I said, handing it to him. "It's yours."

Part II

▼ ▼ ▼ ▼ ▼ ▼ ▼ ▼ ▼

Obalaka Apistikeli
Is Hard To Find

▼ ▼ ▼ ▼ ▼ ▼ ▼ ▼ ▼ ▼ ▼ ▼ ▼ ▼ ▼

*"The dignity of chieftanship was bestowed upon him
who had proved himself worthy by his skill and daring
deeds . . . nor did they wait for opportunities for the display of heroism, but sought perils and toils by which
they might distinguish themselves"*
—Horatio Bardwell Cushman

Suppose you wanted to secure the services of *obalaka
apistikeli*. How does one go about it? Do you hire one? Do
you call the employment office to see if one is available?
Do you look in the *Yellow Pages*?

No one can have need of *obalaka apistikeli* unless that
person is *pelichi bina*. *Pelichi bina* is, by definition, a person who has *obalaka apistikeli*.

It is said of *pelichi bina* that he is worthy of leadership
because *obalaka apistikeli* follows him. It is said that
pelichi bina is free to face what lies ahead because he does
not worry about the backtrail. *Obalaka apistikeli* is always
there.

The Choctaws always went in small bands, which was
the universal custom of their entire race . . . each one
stepped exactly in the tracks of the one who walked before him, while the one in the extreme rear defaced, as
much as possible, their tracks, that no evidence of their
number, or whereabouts might be made known to the
enemy"—Horatio Bardwell Cushman

No one knows where *obalaka apistikeli* might be, except that he is back there somewhere, waiting, watching. It
is said that at night *obalaka apistikeli* circles the *bina*, that

time and again he makes his rounds, disturbing nothing, seen by no one, making the *bina* a safe place to sleep.

It is said that when the men of the *bina* are asleep *obalaka apistikeli* will slip in quietly and take his supper. It is said that *honi bina* always cooks an extra share for him and leaves it near the embers of the fire. It is said that *obalaka apistikeli* always comes and gets the food. It is said that to find the food still there in the morning is a sign of danger on the backtrail.

> "They carry with them a certain thing which they look on as the genius of the party; it is most commonly the stuffed skin of an owl . . . ; they always set him with his head towards the place of destination, and if he should prove to be turned directly contrary, they consider this as portending some very bad omen, and an absolute order to return"—Bernard Romans

> "A bad dream while en route toward the enemy would usually occasion the return home of the dreamer, and if the leader had such a dream, the whole party might turn back. Romans says that the chirp of a species of Motacilla near the camp would have the same effect"—John R. Swanton

Suppose it becomes your turn to do some great deed that the *Okla Chahta* will remember for generations. Would you attempt such a deed without benefit of *tikba pisa*?

Men who have had it fall to them to do some great thing learn that this will be their destiny when they find they have acquired *obalaka apistikeli*. Such men are allowed yet another set of eyes. It is only fair, with the backtrail secure, that they should see far ahead while remaining where they are. That lone hunter walking the woods might be *tikba pisa* for some *pelichi bina*. If so, and if you can see him, you can rest assured that someone you cannot see will soon know all about your presence in the woods.

"To surprise a Choctaw warrior or hunter in the woods—
see him before he saw you—was a feat not easily accom-
plished; in fact, impossible by an experienced white
woodsman, and extremely difficult even by the most experienced"—Horatio Bardwell Cushman

It is for *pelichi bina* each morning to set the course of
the march. It is for *pelichi bina* each evening to choose the
site of the *bina*. It is for *pelichi bina* to know that *tikba pisa*
will find his way back to the *bina* before dark. It is for
pelichi bina to know that *obalaka apistikeli* will find trouble on the backtrail before it can find the *bina*. It is for
pelichi bina each evening and morning to take his squirrel
rifle and scout all around the *bina*, to learn what the terrain might conceal to the casual eye, to know the condition
of the forest in the evening, so that he might see it again in
the morning and know the coming and going of things in
the night. It is said that on his rounds *pelichi bina* confers
with *obalaka apistikeli.*

It is for *tikba pisa* to range far ahead and from side to
side, to learn what lies ahead, and to find his way to his
hot supper and dry bed at the *bina* before dark.

It is for *obalaka apistikeli* to guard the backtrail and be
hard to find.

It is for *honi bina* to tend the fire and cook.

It is for *pelichi bina* to do some great thing.

To His Honor The Governor
▼ ▼ ▼ ▼ ▼ ▼ ▼ ▼ ▼ ▼ ▼ ▼ ▼ ▼ ▼

Received your urgent message this a.m. by way of Brazilian Army courier. Am humbled and honored that you have thought to entrust to me the task of finding and rescuing your kidnapped daughters.

Regret to say I have been commissioned by Her Majesty The Queen to inquire into the whereabouts of one Lord Miltingham, who ascended the Rio Negro from Manaus three years ago on a butterfly collecting expedition and has not been heard from since. Do not know when I will be free to begin the task of finding your daughters, but will do so immediately upon my return.

Am presently six days upriver from Manaus conferring with Captain Ramos and attempting to hire some canoes more suitable to the upriver country. Unfortunately my crew of Drawyas overheard Captain Ramos relating some recent atrocities committed by gold miners upon the Uruquidees, not more than seven leagues upriver, and now the Drawyas say they will not paddle through Uruquidee country lest I provide each of them with a tabnoc root to appease the machinations of the evil spirit Hoorudutau, who overlooks their destines.

The Drawyas have severely tried my patience. Their customs are strange and most unChoctaw. Between the hours of noon and 6 p.m. they insist upon chewing the dried husks of the bauoo bush, which they treat with a liquid of a pale orange color. The odor of the liquid is unpleasant and pervades everything much like the perfume of the North American skunk. While chewing the husks of the bauoo bush the Drawyas fall into a catatonic trance and masturbate incessantly. This makes canoe travel in the afternoon difficult as few of them have mastered the art of paddling one-handed.

In the interests of science I felt compelled to trade with the Drawyas for a quantity of this liquid and some husks, lest this quaint custom become extinct like so many of the native habits of these parts. Now I have the additional logistical problem of transporting forty-three bushels of husks and thirty-seven gallons of liquid downriver and having it stored until such time as I am able to return to Manaus.

The success of our mission hinges upon whether we can reach the Casiquiare Channel before the rainy season overtakes up. As it is late in the season, the vexations with the Drawyas have left me chafing with each delay until my nerves are in such a state that I am hardly my usual cheery self. Were it not for the good humor of my Doogee and the honored beckoning of duty I should think I might turn back.

My Doogee is one of the few people in the outside world who has ever seen the Casiquiare Channel. This in itself seems quite strange to me. The channel has been known as one of the astounding freaks of world geography since it was revealed to the outside world by a German explorer in the 19th century. Much like the famed Unaweep Canyon of western Colorado, it is a stream that flows simultaneously in opposite directions, being something of a natural canal linking the headwaters of the Rio Orinoco of Venezuela with the Rio Negro, and thus the Rio Amazonas, of Brazil. I should think it a natural highway of commerce.

But it has been off limits to the world since the joint agreement between Venezuela and Brazil in 1953. Ostensibly the agreement was reached to protect the remote Iasisus tribe, who are all hemophiliacs. This was necessary because they are a very friendly tribe and the simple contact of shaking hands causes them to bleed to death.

But my Doogee says this is not so, that they are a people of robust constitution and their only affliction as a people is a condition which he describes as a sort of chronic constipation. In their never-ending quest for the relief of their misery my Doogee says that they have lost the ability to stand upright.

Furthermore he maintains that there was a confusion of language between the French Red Cross physicians who examined the Iasisus and the Spanish-speaking Venezuelan and Portuguese-speaking Brazilian officials, and that the affliction of the tribe was improperly reported to be hemophilia, when in fact it is hemorrhoids. The truth of this matter has become a mystery of great suspense, and there is hardly a soul among the entire party who is not desperately eager to reach the Iasisus, except for the Drawyas, who care for nothing except their bauoo bush husks.

It was my Doogee who discovered what is believed to be the last known camp of Lord Miltingham's expedition some two leagues up the Casiquiare, which gave rise to speculation that the expedition unwittingly may have ascended the Casiquiare instead of the Rio Uaupes, as was their known intention.

This prospect so distressed Her Majesty The Queen that she prevailed upon the Venezuelan and Brazilian authorities to lift the restrictions and allow my party to ascend the Casiquiare in search of Lord Miltingham. It seems Her Majesty was informed of the true nature of the affliction of the Iasisus, and she fears that Lord Miltingham, who is her second cousin twice removed, may now be suffering this most unlordly misery.

In view of the urgent seriousness of this mission I fear I must press upriver with all haste. The rainy season is almost upon us, and I must yet find tabnoc roots to appease the Drawyas and prevail upon them to learn to paddle one-handed so that no time be lost. Even then I fear that our relief mission may be in vain for even should we succeed in finding Lord Miltingham I dread to think what might be his condition.

If you can get a message to your daughters tell them to be steadfast and hopeful, that help is on its way, though there must be an unfortunate, unavoidable delay in its arrival until I have done this great thing.

Mother's Mental Illness
▼ ▼ ▼ ▼ ▼ ▼ ▼ ▼ ▼ ▼ ▼ ▼ ▼ ▼ ▼ ▼

Among the most difficult things for a writer to address are private family secrets, things that are not ordinarily made public. Yet, writers have an obligation to deal with difficult issues. One of the most difficult of these is mental illness in one's immediate family.

The sadness of my mother's mental illness, the inconvenience that it has caused me, and the pain of knowing that the mask of sanity which she projects to the world is only something for her to hide behind while she lives an inner life dominated by fantasy are things that I must now share with you.

It's uncomfortable for a son to make public his mother's fantasy life, but perhaps the revelations will bring comfort to others who face similar problems, the simple comfort of knowing that they are not alone.

In Mother's fantasy life, when I finished college, I didn't enter upon a career as a writer. I went into the lawn care business.

I can recall with absolute clarity the moment when Mother's fantasy first manifested itself. I had finished school in mid-year, in December, and had moved back home so I wouldn't have to take a job and could devote my full attention to writing. I was sitting at the breakfast table one fine morning that spring, polishing off a bowl of Cheerios, when, out of the blue, she said the eight words that have forever since been a signal for when her fantasies have taken control of her mind. She said, "When are you going to mow the lawn?"

I said to myself at that very instant, "Poor thing. She thinks I'm in the lawn care business."

I carefully explained to her that I was a full-time freelance writer, that I was writing the great American novel and short stories and poetry and essays and plays and all manner of things, which one day would surely make us all rich, and me famous, and that I had no intention, not then and not at any time in the future, of starting any kind of small business, and certainly not in any kind of service industry.

If you ever face this sort of problem, I can save you a lot of frustration right now. Take my word for it, it is a waste of breath to try to explain anything to one of these crazies. When they are locked in the grip of their fantasy, reason and logic have no place in their mind.

Not only are words to no avail, but hard and fast physical evidence will make no impression upon them. Even, at the end of the second year, when I could show a check from a magazine publisher in the amount of twenty dollars, not even that indisputable evidence of the true nature of my profession could forestall, with the first breath of spring, to be repeated with increasing frequency and heightened stridency for eight solid months, those eight tell tale words that told me that Mother was still consumed by her fantasy.

Of course, I was embarrassed for her, and I did my best to try to keep the thing within the family, fearing that some overzealous mental health official might institute commitment proceedings. I knew that she didn't actually require being institutionalized, that, but for her fantasy, she could function normally in the world.

At least once each year, and some years two or even three times, I would have to get the lawn mower out of the garage and indulge her fantasy. Thus humored, she would be okay for awhile, to all appearances a normal, healthy person. Maybe that's not the healthiest way to treat her sort of problem, and perhaps it might even do more harm than good, but I had no money to consult a psychiatrist and so had to deal with it as best I could.

I now know that the condition is hereditary. Last winter Mother's ninety-one year-old mother moved in with us, and this spring the fantasy manifested itself in Grandmother even before it took hold of Mom. I suspect that this condition might run through that entire side of my family, but I haven't yet pursued any investigations along that line. All I can think about, with two crazies now in the house, is that this year it's going to be a long summer.

Never Again

▼ ▼ ▼ ▼ ▼ ▼ ▼ ▼ ▼ ▼ ▼ ▼ ▼ ▼ ▼ ▼

It was late Friday afternoon, the weekend before Thanksgiving, which meant that deer season would begin the next morning.

I was alone in the living room, idly watching the local news, weather, and sports. Mom and Dad were out in the backyard. My kid brother Delbert was back in his room. My other siblings were scattered all over the planet.

I wasn't watching the news for any particular reason. Certainly deer season was the furthest thing from my mind, until I heard the weather.

We'd been having balmy, 70 degree weather, beautiful days, pleasant nights. But now a blizzard was barrelling down the plains straight toward us. "This will be a major winter storm," said the weatherman. "It's got it all—snow, sleet, freezing rain, bitter arctic wind. We may get a foot or more of snow." It would hit the Oklahoma City area the next day, on Saturday evening, and would hit southeastern Oklahoma late Saturday night. They were warning all creation to take cover.

I tiptoed down the hallway and peeked into Delbert's room to see if by any chance he might be watching the local news on his little TV. He was sitting at his desk reading a book, with a set of stereo headphones clamped to his ears. I could see by the setting on his stereo that he was listening to a local FM rock & roll station, one that didn't even give the time of day, let alone any news or weather.

I looked out in the backyard. Mom and Dad were engaged in a spirited discussion, pointing at the crazyquilt of flower beds and vegetable garden plots the backyard was divided into. I didn't need to hear what they were saying to know what they were talking about: "This space gets just the kind of full sunlight that I need for my creeping phlox," Mother would be saying; and Dad would say, "But that's where I plan to plant my okra next year."

It was an old war, and this skirmish wouldn't be over until nearly time for them to go shopping for groceries, which would get them out of the house during the critical time necessary to get packed and get gone, if Delbert could be enticed into one more outdoor adventure—if he hadn't heard about the change in the weather. Probably Mom and Dad had heard about it.

I popped my head into Delbert's room and said, "Hey!"

He looked around, took the headphones off of his head, and said, "What?"

"Did you know that deer season starts tomorrow morning?" I held my breath. He had vowed never again to follow me off into the woods, and he had meant it, too.

"Deer season?" he said. He looked out the window at the spectacularly beautiful weather. He said, "You want to go?"

He didn't know. *He didn't know.*

"I'm thinking about it," I said. "If we run over right now and get our deer tags, get back and get packed, we can be at Grandpa Crowder's old place by about midnight and camp there at the edge of the woods. Tomorrow we can hike up into the McGee Valley, deer hunt along the way, and camp tomorrow night up on the Potapo. Nobody else will be way off up in there. We're bound to get a deer."

"I loaned out my backpack," he said. "And we ruined that old tent."

"We won't need a tent," I said, walking to the window and looking outside. "We can take that old tarp out in the shed and use it to keep the dew off of us. I've got my backpack, and you can carry my old Marine Corps duffel bag."

A half hour later we were buying our deer tags. By the time we got back home Mom and Dad had left to go shopping. We left them a note telling them where we were going and that we'd be back probably Monday or Tuesday.

While Delbert was throwing his things together I ran over to a buddy's house and borrowed his heavy duty, U.S. Air Force, arctic sleeping bag. Delbert, I noticed, packed a lightweight cotton sleeping bag that didn't even have a waterproof shell.

When he saw me packing my winter hunting coat, gloves, and insulated underwear he looked real thoughtful for a moment, then packed his too, saying, "It might get a bit nippy around daylight."

We packed enough food for a few days, packed a campfire cooking kit, gathered up our deer rifles and ammunition, and left the city well after dark, barely getting away before time for Mom and Dad to get back home.

We talked about deer hunting all the way on the drive down, and I changed stations on the radio every time one of them started to do a news cast. It was after midnight when we pulled up in front of our great-grandfather Crowder's old, abandoned home place, way back in the foothills of the Ouachita Mountains, at the end of the road.

Our great-grandfather had lived to be very near 100 years old, maybe older. We guessed him to be at least 98 when he died, based on the age of his children and on things he could remember about his early life (he didn't know what year he had been born). Recorded by the Dawes Commission as a three-quarter blood Choctaw, he was actually a Chickasaw/Choctaw mixed blood, descended from a white man named Eli Crowder, who settled among the Choctaws, and intermarried, probably sometime in the 1780s or 1790s, who fathered large families of mixed bloods, first by a Choctaw wife, then by a Chickasaw wife, from whom our great-grandfather was descended (though the Chickasaw blood had been forgotten until some of the family got to digging around in old history books).

Eli Crowder and his in-laws had been a part of Pushmataha's 800-man Choctaw army that fought engagements with a faction of the Creeks in the War of 1812, where Eli won the name "Muscokubi" (Creek Killer) in an episode told at some length in H.B. Cushman's *History of the Choctaw, Chickasaw, and Natchez Indians* (1899). Some of Eli's descendants became prominent in tribal politics during the 19th century, one of them becoming one of the principal interpreters in the nation. But our great-grandfather preferred the solitude at the edge of the McGee Creek wilderness, where he and his son, our great-uncle Bunnie, lived for most of the 20th century. They had finally died one winter, within a few weeks of one another, a few years earlier. Our father had been their favorite relative. Dad practically lived with them, off and on, when he was growing up. Dad said Grandpa Crowder was a white-haired old man when he first met him.

As we pulled up and parked, even by moonlight Granddad's old place looked changed almost beyond recognition. Planning was well advanced to build a dam on the McGee, and people who specialize in ruining remote areas were already at work. Somebody had bulldozed all the timber across the road in front of Granddad's place. We had intended to camp in that timber.

Now we could see for a quarter of a mile to the north across the new pasture, all the way to the new treeline which we knew was where the land fell away down a steep mountainside to the McGee below. We decided to hike across the new pasture to the treeline to make camp. It was not quite 2 A.M. when we crawled into our sleeping bags and fell asleep, under a bright canopy of stars, the kind of sight that's simply unavailable in the light-polluted atmosphere of a city.

We were up at first light, in time to cook a big breakfast and be packed up and ready to go by the time it was light enough to see how to hunt. Deer season had now begun, so we eased our way into the woods, hunting as we went.

Looking back across the new pasture at Granddad's old place I could barely believe it was such a short distance away. Where we had camped was about halfway from Granddad's house to the McGee. As a kid, it had been a pure wilderness adventure to go to the McGee. The world seemed suddenly smaller and not nearly as interesting. There had been a maze of different trails through the pine forest leading from Granddad's house to different places on the McGee. It seemed it had taken half my life to learn those trails, and they passed through many different environments, different visual experiences, different places. Now anyone could find his way across the pasture, and it all looked pretty much the same.

Neither me or Delbert could figure out exactly where we had camped in relation to that old network of trails, and rather than cast around trying to find one of the old trails we just headed down through the timber on the steep, rocky hillside. We came out on the McGee a little upstream of where we usually did, but that was alright, as we had to go upstream quite a bit to wade the river at the shoals.

I noticed that Delbert was having some trouble trying to find a comfortable way to carry the duffel bag, with it's single heavy strap. It didn't work very well trying to sling it over one shoulder, the strap wasn't long enough to sling it across his back, and it was too heavy and bulky to try to carry by its hand strap. Carrying it up on top of his shoulder seemed to be about the only way to do it, which didn't look like much fun. In fact, it looked downright awkward, as he was also trying to carry his deer rifle and a chopping axe.

When we got to the shoals just below the mouth of Crooked Creek, at the exact spot where the McGee Creek dam now sits, we met a fellow on horseback wading the river coming toward us. When he got to our side he danced his pony around a little bit and said he had missed a good shot at a big buck about daylight up near the mouth of the Potapo. When we told him that's where we were heading he wished us luck, saying as far as he'd seen we'd have the whole woods to ourselves.

The river gurgled and splashed as it raced through the rocky shoals. Spring-fed and clear and not quite knee deep, we pulled off our boots and socks and rolled our pants legs up to wade it. The day was already warm, with bright sunshine, and the mountain valley was sprinkled here and there with the very last of the autumn colors.

After crossing the river, Delbert stood drinking in the sights. He said, "You know, this is how it ought to be, two brothers out doing the things that brothers ought to do. I'm really glad we made this trip."

I nearly broke down and told him about the blizzard right then and there. Just hearing him talk like that brought a catch to my throat, and it was all I could do to keep from getting all misty eyed.

He asked me if I remembered the time that summer after we had moved up to western Colorado, when I had only been in college up there for a year or two and he and our kid brother Ernie were just little brats, when we went backpacking up the side of the Grand Mesa that time with Billy Burch, up the Kannah Creek trail, and after we got camped that night it came one of the heaviest rainstorms they'd ever had up there. Did I remember that, and did I remember how we'd just about gotten situated that night where we could sleep about half-dry under that rain tarp when that big American Water Spaniel of ours came crawling under the tarp with us and got us all soaking wet before we could stop him.

Yes, I said, I remembered that, as I scuffed my boots on the ground and then studied the marks I'd made in the dirt, and wasn't it a surprise when it started raining, and rained hard all that night and all the next day, and it had been such pretty weather and all.

Ten minutes later I had a stroke of inspiration. Our plan, after wading the McGee, was to head west for about a half-mile, following the trace of an old logging road until, way up on the hillside, there was an old fenceline that led straight to the mouth of the Potapo about a mile away to the north. That fenceline crossed some little creeks that fed into the McGee to our right. It occurred to me that on that route we would come to another old fenceline that would connect with our fence at right angles, coming from the west. If I remembered right it would join our fence in a dense stand of pines, and it might be possible to get old Delbert off on that other fenceline, heading west instead of north, heading out of the watershed of the McGee Valley, heading toward the Muddy Boggy River, where the little creeks we would cross would be flowing to our left toward the Boggy, rather than to our right toward the McGee.

I wondered how long it might take old Delbert, who knew the way to the mouth of the Potapo about as well as I did, to figure out that something had gone wrong. It was not far to the Potapo, but it was several miles to the Muddy Boggy. If a fellow was concentrating hard on deer hunting he might not notice the change in direction. I wondered if I could get him all the way to the Boggy before he figured out where we were.

After wading the McGee we followed the trace of that old logging road up the hillside, came to that old fenceline and started following it north. Pretty soon I saw that dense clump of pines up ahead where the other fence would be joining ours.

I said, "Hey, we ought to hunt that cover pretty close, don't you think? How about we get over on the other side of the fence and you slip out there a ways, and I'll ease along here by the fence, and maybe one of us will flush out a deer to where the other one can get a shot."

Sure enough, we climbed over the fence and Delbert eased off out into the woods about fifty yards. I got a little bit ahead of him and started angling toward the west. He used me as a bearing, thinking I was walking along the fenceline, and I gradually got him headed due west just about the time I came upon that other fence. Pretty soon we ran out of that clump of pines, and he came over to where I was, and we proceeded down that fenceline, hiking straight out of the Valley of the McGee.

It was uncanny how that one old fenceline looked like the other one, and the terrain was all pretty much the same. I noticed when we topped the little rise that separated the McGee watershed from the Muddy Boggy, but Delbert was intent on his deer hunting and was paying no attention at all to where we were going.

We slowed the pace considerably. We did some still hunting through the woods, sometimes on one side of the fence, sometimes on the other side. Time ticked away. It was getting on toward the middle of the day, and we had already gone far enough to have gotten to the mouth of the Potapo, when we crossed the first little creek. It was flowing off to our left, off toward the Muddy Boggy as pretty as you please, but Delbert didn't give it any mind.

We'd gone about another half-mile before Delbert said, "Shouldn't we already be at the mouth of the Potapo by now?"

"Well," I said, looking all around, "it does seem like we've been at it for awhile, doesn't it? I've kind of lost track of time and distance the way we've been concentrating on deer hunting so much."

The sun was high overhead, standing in the noon post, so we decided to stop and heat up some soup. We'd hardly gotten started again when we came to a place where the fence went right through the middle of a bunch of tall boulders.

Delbert, standing in the middle of the boulders, looking up all around, said, "I don't remember anyplace like this."

On down the trail we came to another little creek. Delbert stopped and stared at it for a long time. He said, "Am I all turned around, or what? This thing's flowing off in the wrong direction."

By then the valley of the McGee was far behind us. We were up near the top of the watershed that separated the Muddy Boggy drainage, to the south and west, from the valley of the Potapo, which was just the other side of a little rise to the north. The water in that little creek was barely a trickle, but it was definitely flowing downhill, and that was definitely to our left, and Delbert definitely stared at it for a long time.

He said, "Something is not right."

I said, "You don't suppose somebody moved the mouth of the Potapo on us do you?"

We finally decided we must have come upon one of those little creeks that went first one way and then another, and we just didn't remember it.

I said, "I'll bet the next time we cross it, it'll be flowing the other way."

But he knew those big boulders were not on the trail to the mouth of the Potapo. He said, "Man, this is spooky."

Another quarter of a mile brought us to another creek. It was a little bit bigger than the other one, and there was no doubt about which way it was flowing either.

"We're lost," he said. "I don't believe it. We should have come to the mouth of the Potapo a long time ago. I don't know where we are, but we're nowhere near the mouth of the Potapo."

It was a complete mystery, and we spent a considerable period of time discussing it. Finally, Delbert said, "I think we've been going toward the west."

The sun was beginning to dip toward the west, and it was becoming more and more obvious that we were hiking straight toward the sunset.

I said, "Do you suppose we might have been concentrating on deer hunting so hard that we got on the wrong fenceline somewhere?"

We decided to give it one more try down the fenceline. About another quarter of a mile brought us to another little creek, and it was flowing off in the wrong direction just like all the others.

"This is as far as I'm going," said Delbert. "If we camp here at least maybe we'll be able to find our way back. Dad never will stop laughing if he finds out we got off up here and got lost."

The little creek had just enough water flowing in it to use it for camp water, so we followed it downstream until we found a good place to camp. We pitched camp and then went out deer hunting until it got nearly dark.

We hadn't seen a deer all day, and we weren't real sure

where we were, but that didn't dampen our spirits. It was a beautiful evening, and a big supper cooked over a campfire tasted pretty good.

We sat around drinking coffee, just enjoying the evening and the campfire, until finally we spread out that old tarp, rolled out our sleeping bags on top of it, and bedded down.

We lay there awhile, just gazing up at the stars and talking. We'd almost dropped off to sleep when we heard geese honking.

"Do you hear that?" said Delbert.

"I sure do," I said.

Before long they came flying directly over us. They were flying so low we could almost reach up and touch them. They were straggled out in the most ragged-looking V shape you ever did see, a bunch of dead-tired geese barely able to flap their wings, hollering and complaining and protesting, making the most awful racket. It took a long time for all of them to finally pass over us.

Delbert snorted. "Ha," he said. "Uncle Bunnie said when you see a flock of tired geese flying low like that it's a sure sign there's a blue norther right behind them. But look at it. There's not a cloud in the sky."

The Uncle Bunnie Delbert was referring to was our dad's youngest brother, who lived not far from Grandfather Crowder's old place. It was one absolutely beautiful, balmy night, and it was still warm, well after dark. We had a good laugh about our Uncle Bunnie's cornpone Choctaw country wisdom and then dropped off to sleep.

We woke up an hour or two later with a cold, hard, driving rain hitting us in the face. The sky had turned pitch black, and the campfire was nothing but embers, so we had to turn on a flashlight to see how to get the tarp out from under our sleeping bags, throw it over them for a shelter, and crawl back into the sleeping bags beneath the tarp.

Delbert's cotton sleeping bag got wet before he could get it covered up, and we both got wet running around getting things situated. I was able to get snuggled up again nice and cozy in that heavy, waterproof, arctic sleeping bag, and would have been able to drop right back off to sleep if Delbert hadn't started complaining.

He complained about the holes in the tarp. It did have holes in it, about as big as your hand, every few feet all the way across it. He said about all the tarp was doing was collecting the water so it could run down the holes and get him soaking wet.

Then the rain turned to freezing rain, with a howling, shrieking wind, and he stopped complaining about being wet and started complaining about being cold.

The next thing I knew he'd gotten up and gotten dressed and was building a bonfire to end all bonfires. By then the freezing rain had turned to heavy snow.

The first bonfire he built didn't work very well. He built it over on the other side of the creek up against some big rocks where it was a little bit sheltered from the wind. It burned well enough alright, and the pitchy old pine limbs he piled up made a big, hot fire that threw a lot of heat. But he failed to notice that the flat slab of rock he built it on top of had fissures and fractures running all the way through it. When the fire got real hot, and when those fractured pieces of rock had expanded as far as they could expand, they exploded up out of those cracks all in one big boom.

I woke up to what sounded like a mortar attack, with fire raining down everywhere and Delbert running for his life, with the explosion scattering rocks and bonfire and blazing limbs from hell to breakfast.

I told him I would appreciate it if he could make a little less racket, that some people were trying to sleep.

I drifted in and out of sleep all night long, waking up now and then when he would come in from the woods dragging a bunch of firewood.

When I woke up at daylight it was still snowing hard. There was at least a foot of it on the ground, and it had drifted three or four feet deep in places. The wind was howling out of the north at least twenty or thirty miles an hour. Delbert was standing in front of his bonfire, stamping his feet, flapping his arms. He looked about as frazzled as a man can get.

I got up and got dressed quickly. I said, "This may be just the lucky break we've been needing. The one thing you can count on on a day like today is that the deer will be someplace where there's some shelter from this wind."

He just glared at me. He said, "If you think I'm going anywhere except straight to the car, you're crazy."

We had some coffee and cooked breakfast. After he'd finished eating he felt better. He said, "Where do you figure they'd be on a day like today?"

I said I wouldn't be surprised if we were a little bit south of the Potapo, about a mile, maybe, and if he would remember, along the south side of the Potapo were some steep hillsides, almost cliffs, with some deep cuts in them that ran way back up in the hills for about a half mile. Down in those cuts, out of the wind, was where I figured the deer would be.

I pointed upstream on the little creek we were camped on. I said I'd bet it wasn't more than a quarter of a mile upstream to the crest of the watershed and just the other side of it was probably the top of one of those cuts. In this high wind the deer wouldn't hear us coming, and they'd be upwind of us. We might both get a nice buck.

He wanted to know how I expected us to carry out a deer through the snow drifts. "It's been all I can do," he said, "to carry in firewood."

I said if we got a deer we could field-dress it, hang it up in a tree to freeze, and come back and get it when the weather cleared.

The more we talked about it the more we liked the plan, and Delbert was ready to do some deer hunting by the time we got all packed up and broke camp.

We hiked upstream to the fenceline and left our packs there. We stacked them almost on top of the top strand of the wire, as the snow had drifted almost all the way over the fence.

Not long after crossing the fence we crossed over the watershed and found a little depression that soon turned into a deeper and deeper gully, heading northeast.

We soon found ourselves descending into a deeper and deeper canyon. When we saw a thick stand of evergreens up ahead we eased up close to it. We settled in to wait and watch, figuring we had a pretty good deer stand.

We were out of the wind, but the cold was miserable, a damp, humid cold. The longer we sat there the colder we got. The temperature must have been at least down in the teens. Before long our teeth began to chatter.

"I think stopping was a mistake," I finally whispered.

"I think not going back to the car was a mistake," Delbert whispered back.

"I think you're right," I said.

We stood up.

Deer exploded all around us. There were so many white flags bobbing up and down in so many different directions that all we could do was stand there, dumbfounded, and stare.

"Well," said Delbert, when the last one had disappeared, "we found the deer. I'm not sure where, exactly, we found them, somewhere in Oklahoma, maybe, but we did find them."

Hours later, after slogging our way through the snow drifts, feeling the constant bite of that howling wind, we finally retraced our route all the way back to the McGee. It was still snowing hard.

Standing there at the edge of the water, not wanting to wade out into it with our boots on, and not wanting to take our boots off either, Delbert was in a foul mood. On the way back he'd pretty much worked out the little bit of trickery about those two fencelines in that dense clump of pines and was beginning to have his suspicions about the weather.

Neither one of us could quite work up enough nerve to take off our boots before wading the river, so we had to climb that long, steep hillside to get on up toward Grand-dad's old place with wet, squishy, freezing feet.

It didn't help any that the lock on the car door was frozen full of ice and had to be thawed out with a cigarette lighter before we could get it open.

"Well," I said, "at least we can drive over to Uncle Bun-nie's and get dried out and warmed up before heading back. I'll bet he's already got a deer."

Delbert wasn't much company on the way over to our uncle's house. He just slumped down in the car seat, shaking his head, saying, "Never again."

Roads To Nowhere

▼ ▼ ▼ ▼ ▼ ▼ ▼ ▼ ▼ ▼ ▼ ▼ ▼ ▼ ▼ ▼

Sleet was rattling the window panes on a January night in Oklahoma City as I pored over one U.S. Geological Survey map after another. Our long-cherished deer hunting woods at the western edge of the Ouachita Mountains in southeastern Oklahoma, where my Choctaw ancestors had hunted for generations, were being buried beneath McGee Creek Reservoir. I was trying to find a new place where we could hunt during the fall deer season.

I finally found it, in the upper watershed of the Kiamichi River, in the Ouachita National Forest of southern LeFlore County in southeastern Oklahoma, a completely hidden valley, nestled along the side of Winding Stair Mountain, tucked away behind Lenox Ridge.

From out in the big valley, several miles away, where the highway followed the course of the Kiamichi River, at an elevation of 700 feet, it would be impossible to tell that there was any kind of a gap behind Lenox Ridge. Only a few locals would be likely to know the place was there.

The little hidden valley was long and narrow, less than a mile wide and about four miles long, running east and west. Through the middle of it flowed Sycamore Creek, ranging in elevation from near 1,200 feet at its upper, eastern, end to about 900 feet at its western end, where the creek turned abruptly south and flowed through a deep, narrow gap in Lenox Ridge, which allowed it to flow on down to the Kiamichi River, about five miles away. The north side of that little valley rose steeply, to about 2,300 feet, straight up the side of Winding Stair Mountain. The

73

south side rose almost as steeply, to about 1,500 feet, to the top of Lenox Ridge.

Best of all, it was not that easy to get to. The forest service road leading into it came from far to the east through wild backcountry. That little hidden valley was near the end of the line, about as far back in the boonies as we could get.

That August, Dad and I made a swing through that part of the state. We introduced ourselves to Ralph Rose, the local game warden. When we told him we'd hoped to find someplace along the Kiamichi River to set out a trotline, he gave us the key to his gate and let us camp on his place down by the river.

When I mentioned the little valley behind Lenox Ridge, his eyes lit up, and as he talked about it you could tell it was a special place. He said it was managed for deer and turkey and small game, with food plots down along the creek and wildlife watering ponds up on Lenox Ridge.

The next evening, just before dusk, Dad and I drove through that little valley. Our progress was impeded for several minutes by two fawns dancing and playing in the dusty forest service road, while their nervous mother watched from behind a clump of brush along the creek.

In the long, cool shadows, the campsite we found proved to be ideal. There was plenty of spring-fed water in the creek.

Driving back home we knew we had found our place. It was, in a way, familiar country. For many years, at intervals, from the time I was very young, we had taken my great-grandfather Crowder and my great-uncle Bunnie Crowder to the Indian hospital at Talihina for treatment. They had both died while I was in college, and Dad and I had not been back in that part of the country for awhile. It felt good to be there again. In the 1930s Dad had driven a truck all through the upper valleys of the Ouachita Mountains when he was in the Civilian Conservation Corps. He knew the mountains the way they used to be.

I decided to hunt that little hidden valley during bow

season. As the weeks went by, I practiced with my two-wheel compound bow. Standing on the roof of the house, I sank arrow after arrow into a bale of hay in the backyard.

I was camped on Sycamore Creek for opening day of the October bow season. By scouting around on the steep slopes of Winding Stair Mountain, I found a little rill that dropped into a small canyon, splashing down over the drop-off as a small waterfall. The area was heavily timbered, but at the head of the little canyon, where the waterfall splashed into a small pool of water, was a sandy area thick with deer tracks. Right at the top of the waterfall was a knarled, stunted pine, nearly completely hidden by the tops of other trees thrusting up from down near the pool of water.

By late afternoon I was standing in the branches of that knarled pine. The distance to the sandy area beside the pool of water down below was almost exactly the same as from the roof of the house to that bale of hay in the backyard.

I wore complete camo gear, including hat, gloves, and face cream. I smelled like a skunk. Two little drops of a commercial chemical concoction, odorless in themselves, became instant skunk when mixed together on the bottom of my boots. This did not endear me to the proprietors of local commercial establishments whenever I went to buy supplies, but it completely covered my human scent.

Several times my pulse rate picked up at the sound of something tromping through the dry, crackling leaves. But each time it proved to be a squirrel. Then, late in the afternoon, came a "tromp, tromp, tromp" far too heavy-footed to be a squirrel.

The sound was coming from directly behind me, from higher up the mountainside, but it kept getting nearer and nearer.

It took all the willpower I could muster to keep from trying to turn my head. The waiting was nearly unbearable. I was thinking state record archery whitetail deer, when five wild turkeys came slowly into view, walking single file down the hillside.

They were making an enormous amount of noise in the dry leaves, something they were obviously aware of. As they stopped on the rim of the little canyon, at just about eye level with me, and not more than ten yards away, they began to scratch around and peck at the ground beneath the leaves. But never did all five of them have their heads down at once. In fact, each individual was a study in nervous motion. Completely paranoid, they spent more time looking around than pecking the ground.

I didn't dare so much as breathe, let alone attempt to move. It was fall turkey season, but not in Leflore County. Even if the county had been a part of the fall hunt, there is no way I would have been able to get untangled among the branches to make the necessary half turn for a shot. There were tree limbs in the way, and the turkeys were just too close.

After awhile they wandered off, the sound of their tromping through the dry leaves gradually dying away.

I was aware of having experienced an almost magical, mystic moment, one that might never come again, and I thanked the seclusion and secretiveness of my little hidden valley for it.

That night before falling asleep, I watched the stars for a long time and relived those moments over and over again.

The next day I decided to check out Lenox Ridge. I found a tall pine tree beside one of the small ponds on the ridge and climbed it.

I found a comfortable bow stand on one of the lower limbs, but since it was still early, I decided to climb higher in the tree to take in the view.

I had climbed nearly to the top of the tree when Ralph Rose, the game warden, pulled up in his truck. He got out and started walking toward the little pond.

I said, "Howdy."

Ralph stopped. He looked all around. He stood still for a long time, looking, listening, looking some more.

Finally, he shrugged it off and walked on to the pond.

I said, "Howdy."

This time he *knew* he had heard something. He was looking and listening in earnest when finally I said, "Up here."

It took him awhile to spot me. When he finally did, he grinned. He said, "Boy, you really disappeared up there."

Then he saw my bow. He said, "What's your killing range with that thing?"

I said, "About twenty-five yards."

He said, "You're higher off the ground than that."

I climbed down and we talked awhile. I told him about the turkeys.

Back in the tree, I counted eighteen squirrels that afternoon coming in to drink at the pond, seventeen gray squirrels and one big, fat, fox squirrel. Five of the squirrels were in one group, four little ones and the mother. They were like the Keystone Cops the way they frolicked and chased one another around. But all the squirrels, even the little ones, approached the pond very cautiously, sneaking down to drink, and not lingering near the water any more than necessary.

Late in the day a bellowing hound dog and a small, fat mutt came by chasing a whitetail buck. They passed within seventy-five yards of the tree, the little fat dog trailing along silently quite a distance behind the hound dog, both of them well behind the deer. They chased the deer nearly out of hearing up the valley and then came back almost exactly where they had passed by the first time. They were still at it as darkness approached.

The next day I decided to climb Winding Stair Mountain, just for the sheer joy of the climb, leaving my gear at camp. It was steep going, but the heavily timbered, rugged wildness of the place was more than compensation.

I had climbed to a point high above Lenox Ridge, and I knew I must be nearing the top of the mountain, when I found the first beer can. Then I found another one, and then dozens and dozens of them.

And not just beer cans, but all kinds of trash, candy wrappers, pop bottles, an old mattress, piles of complete and utter yuk. Then I heard traffic, the unmistakable whine of automobiles whizzing by at high speed. Then I heard voices.

I climbed up onto a modern two-lane highway. A fairly high volume of traffic was flying by at a high rate of speed. But not all of it.

Half a dozen vehicles were pulled off at a scenic over-look, right beside where I had climbed up. More than a dozen people were milling around. Kids were throwing rocks over the edge and people were taking pictures. Some of them had binoculars.

"Look, Daddy," said one kid. "Somebody is camped down there."

I looked too. Somebody was camped down there. I was camped down there.

"Yeah," said the father, looking through binoculars. "Boy, he's got quite a set-up."

With nothing but the naked eye I could see my camp-fire, my bedroll. I asked the man if I could look through his binoculars. I could see my coffee pot, my frying pan, the socks and undershorts I'd rinsed out and hung up to dry.

"Boy," said the man. "Who'd want to camp right out in the open like that? If it was me I'd at least want a little pri-vacy."

By discreetly asking around, I discovered I was stand-ing on the Talimena Scenic Drive and that the fall foliage tour was in full swing. I learned that just a short distance down the highway was a road that led down into the val-ley. I realized with chagrin that this was the extension of the road that I had used, from the opposite direction, when I had entered the valley.

"Where does this highway go?" I asked.

I was told that it doesn't go anywhere. It's just a scenic drive, and a long one at that, along the crest of Winding

Stair Mountain, and other mountains, from near Talihina, Oklahoma, to near Mena, Arkansas.

"If it weren't for this highway, this whole area would just be going to waste," I was told by one lady, who obviously thought it was a splendid idea.

I thought of the miles and miles of habitat destroyed by the highway itself, and the many more square miles affected by the instant access, and I was appalled. I found out later that the scenic drive was an early 1960's Congressional boondoggle, and that President Kennedy had cut the ribbon at the opening ceremony.

That little valley was never the same after that. From camp, now that I knew where to look, I could see the glint of reflected light off the windshields of the cars at the scenic overlook. And while I had to give the wildlife commission high marks for good management in the face of such intrusion, it was just never the same again.

I packed up and left. At home, I found my map error. I had overlooked a little red and white segmented line at the upper edge of the USGS map. Even worse, I realized that Dad and I had driven along a portion of that highway in August, though we hadn't been aware of what it was.

We camped there for deer gun season in November, but it just wasn't the same, and even though our party took two deer, we've never been back.

Sanctuary

▼ ▼ ▼ ▼ ▼ ▼ ▼ ▼ ▼ ▼ ▼ ▼ ▼ ▼ ▼ ▼

I was a fool to be standing at the edge of the water. Only a few feet from me rocks half the size of truck tires were being tossed around in the current like so many ping pong balls in a bingo hopper. But the roar of the water was mesmerizing, and it held me at its edge.

I learned that day that tons of melting snow can turn an ankle deep creek into an angry river, that big rocks can sound like an explosion when they smash together, and that water can rush by at such great speed that it roars.

It was all a surprise to me. I'd expected to jog up the mountainside, from down about 6,500 feet, to up around 9 or 10,000 feet, to wherever the snow, up in the Blue Spruce belt, got to be too deep to slog through it.

It was my valley, a big basin, actually, nestled up in the high country. It was mine because I had worshipped it with my feet in all seasons, in all weather, except, until that day, during the height of the spring runoff.

It had so many different parts. Vertically, the mountainside was a succession of different ecological zones, from arid brush country, to Quaking Aspen, to towering Blue Spruce, from rabbits to mule deer to elk.

The trail was a steep one, until you got up to about 8,000 feet. There, you stood on the lip of a big basin, with the mountain falling away behind you, and with the bowl of the valley spread out before you. Beaver ponds were everywhere, and little creeks, and everywhere that there was water there were Rainbow Trout. Who wouldn't love it?

80

Through the middle of the basin the largest creek had carved a gorge. Its northern rim was a cliff, but the south side stopped just short of being too steep to get down to the trout water, down to where, in the narrow, pine studded bottom of the gorge, you could almost believe no one else had ever been.

By luck, my family had moved from Oklahoma to the mountains the summer before I entered college. For five years that high basin valley was the place I fled to, whenever school took a break, or when a long weekend offered itself, or, sometimes, when I was supposed to be somewhere else. I wanted to know everything there was to know about it. Practically all of the valley was displayed on one 7 1/2 minute quadrangle from the U.S. Geological Survey. I carried that quadrangle everywhere, when I went away to school, whenever I went to visit the kinfolks in Oklahoma, on a trip throughout South America. The valley was always with me. I got to where I didn't need the map, could sketch a map of my own, showing all the creeks, the trails, the secret places.

I spent part of one summer up on the mountain above the basin, skidding logs behind a bulldozer, living with the operator in a small trailer, sitting in the shadows each evening glassing the elk down below with a spotting scope. I spent the last several weeks before heading off to Marine Corps Officer Candidate School by jogging from the foot of the mountain to the top; and when I arrived at the training camp, down close to sea level at Quantico, VA, they found that I could run forever.

And then one day, I don't know how, cannot comprehend how, more than twenty years had gone by since I'd last been in that valley. I was standing at a magazine rack in a supermarket, a backpacking magazine open in my hands, one that showed the detailed, proposed route of a transcontinental backpack trail for its section that crossed the Rocky Mountains, a route that would take the trail through the middle of my beloved high basin valley.

I went back to the valley then, to see it one more time

before the rest of the world began flooding through it. When I got to Colorado an old college friend drove me up above the valley on a Forest Service road to where you could park, walk a few hundred yards, and come to a point where you could look down into it.

It was a wasted trip. It was worse than just a wasted trip. The valley looked the same, it looked magnificent. But the aging little fat man, gasping and wheezing from too many years of tobacco abuse, who had to stop twice to rest, just to get back up the gentle slope to the car, was pathetic. The proposed route of that backpack trail could be moved a hundred miles and it wouldn't make any difference. It's not my valley anymore.

Part III

▼ ▼ ▼ ▼ ▼ ▼ ▼ ▼ ▼

Great Walks and Great Talks
in Choctaw History
▼ ▼ ▼ ▼ ▼ ▼ ▼ ▼ ▼ ▼ ▼ ▼ ▼ ▼ ▼ ▼

Many years ago, not long after the removal of most of the southern nations to new homes west of the Mississippi, and some time after many of them had gathered to sign the treaty of Camp Holmes, the Choctaws invited ballplayers from a number of nations to gather for a time of feasting and sport, as had been their custom, at intervals, in their old homelands. One evening during the gathering the Choctaws offered to entertain their guests with the recitation of some great talk from Choctaw history.

Now, among the ballplayers present were many members of the Muscogee Confederation, some Arbeka, some Hitchitee, some Euchee, and several others, who, all being good Creeks, met the prospect of receiving instruction in oratory from the Choctaws with a great yawning indifference.

It was not that the Choctaws had not made many great talks, they told the ballplayers of the other nations, it was simply that if the evening's entertainment was to consist of stories of great events from the Choctaw past, the Choctaws should not be so modest as to restrict the subject merely to their great talks, when there were so many great events, such as some of their great walks, which might also make a good talk.

After some discussion the ballplayers agreed that they would like to hear the Creeks tell of some great Choctaw walk and then hear the Choctaws tell some great Choctaw talk.

For their telling of a great Choctaw walk, the Creeks,

after conferring among themselves, chose to tell the story of the great Choctaw walk of the winter of 1785–86, when two renowned Choctaw chiefs, Yockonahoma, Great Medal Mingo of Soonacoha, and Tobocoh, Great Medal Mingo of Congetoo, and their entire escort, thirty-one Choctaw honored men and experienced warriors altogether, walked all the way from the headwaters of the Tombigbee River to the big whiskey party hosted by their new East Coast treaty friends at Hopewell on the banks of the Keowee, near Seneca Old Town in the Carolinas, where they finally arrived, ragged and barefoot and very late, to get big drunk and sign their first treaty with the Americans, the treaty of January 3, 1786.

Why, the assembled ballplayers were asked, do the Creeks consider this to have been among the greatest walks in all of Choctaw history? It was a great walk because, at their first night's encampment, the Creeks had stolen all of their horses.

Now, the Choctaws had intended to tell a great talk of Aiahokatubbee, the legendary *Tichou mingo* for Moshulatubbee, Great Medal Mingo of Okla Tanap. But, after hearing the talk of the Creeks, and after all of the assembled ballplayers had finally stopped laughing, they chose instead to tell a great talk of Moshulatubbee's uncle, delivered upon the occasion of the second treaty between the Choctaws and the Americans:

"I understand our great father, General Washington, is dead, and that there is another beloved man appointed in his place, and that he is a well wisher of us. Our old brothers, the Chickasaws, have granted a road from Cumberland as far south as our boundary. I grant a continuance of that road which may be straightened. But the old path is not to be thrown away entirely, and a new one made. We are informed by these three beloved men that our father, the President, has sent us a yearly present of which we know nothing. Another thing our father, the President, has promised, without our asking, is that he would send women among us to teach our women to spin and weave.

These women may first go among our half-breeds. We wish the old boundary which separates us and the whites to be marked over. We came here sober, to do business, and wish to return sober and request therefore that the liquor we are informed our friends have provided for us may remain in the store." —Homassatubbee, Great Medal Mingo of Ahe Pat Okla, 1801, Fort Adams.

Uncle

That drunken Indian on the train back in 1919
was my uncle, my great-uncle
fresh from the big war
Dad said he could always tell when he was drunk
by the way he sat his horse

He'd get drunk and get mean
Wouldn't hardly anybody have anything to do with him
when he was drinking

I never saw him drunk
I knew him about as well as anybody
so I have trouble imagining what they're talking about
when they talk about him drunk

I saw him probably forty times a year
for about ten years running
slept many a night in his house
He never so much as said a mean word to me

They say he went off to do his drinking
They say he'd be gone until the money ran out
come home in a hell of a shape
take two, three weeks to get over being sick

That's what they say
but I never saw him sick

Dad said he saw him sick lots of times
said he saw him near death
said he knew it would be the drinking
that would kill him

He was my oldest uncle
brother of my grandmother
great-uncle to a grand-nephew
whose father married a white woman
and who had no elder Choctaw maternal uncle
to teach him

I think that is why
I never saw him drunk

▼

Born There

My grandmother was born near the Muddy Boggy
Her Choctaw allotment was there
My great-grandfather was born there
His Choctaw allotment was there
My great-great-grandfather was born there
His mother and father were herded there
In the dead of winter
Walking
At the point of a United States Army bayonet

We no longer yearn for *Nanih Waiya*
Time took care of that
It was their plan
Move us, get us out of their way
In time we would forget our old home
We have forgotten it
Home became the Muddy Boggy

My father was born near the Muddy Boggy
I was born there
But none of my siblings were born there
They were born in the city
They know the river
Dad saw to that
Trotlines when the weather begins to warm
Hot, dusty blackberry thickets
Deer when the persimmons ripen
Swamp rabbits in the snow
They know it
But they were not born there
And their children have not been born there
Few of my cousins were born there

And few of their children have been born there
In a short time
My grandmother's people may no longer know the river
Whose plan was that?

The big map at the Oklahoma highway department has a
        symbol
The symbol is on the Muddy Boggy
Calculated to do the most damage
Where the two main tributaries meet
The symbol is a dam site
When that symbol becomes a dam
Who will mourn the loss?
Who will know the loss?
Who will care?
Whose plan was that?

We must go back to old Boggy
We must live there, fish there, be there
We must make fat babies to be born there
That is my plan

▼

Dear Old Fishing Buddy . . .
Dear Grannie B.

▼▼▼▼▼▼▼▼▼▼▼▼▼▼▼▼

April 6, 1970
Mr Don Birchfield
P.O. Box 978
Leadville. Colorado. 80461

Dear old fishing Buddy,

I try and ansuer your letter after so long always glad to hear from you I dont feal so good I took a cold But I still dragen sure hop you are OK Wall your poor old dad had to go Back to the steel work he sure did hate to he started today he working at Wheatlan it sure has Been Bad weather hear it Rain and snow Saturday nearly all day wall old Bun sure is catchen the cat fish out Boggy now Ed and family was daun thair Easter said he had caught lat Big one wall how is Bill getting along By now fine I hope wall the Revivle started last night your mother and tuins came home yesterday from atoka Been doun week Delbert says he having time keeping the girls off him all the rest doing very well thay getting over the flue all I get to do is set in the house and peace quilts I peace 6 tops and on my 7 one to cold wet to plant my garden yet I seen Elmer Wednesday he pertty good But cant work yet still going to the Doctor pee wee said tell you hi we are all thinking about you wall I dont no much to write I say so long and love and Best wishes to you from Granny B.

▼

BISHINIK, The Official Monthly Publication of the Choctaw Nation of Oklahoma, Durant, Oklahoma, July, 1992, page 8.

Ophelia Crowder Birchfield

Ophelia Crowder Birchfield, an original enrollee, age 96, died December 24, 1991. Burial was in Farris Community Cemetery.

She was a great-granddaughter of Patsy Goins and Eli Crowder, who settled among the Choctaws before the War of 1812. He married first Margaret Durant and then Patsy Goins, fathering large families with each wife. He fought under Pushmataha's command in the War of 1812, earning the name "Muscokubi" (Creek Killer) in a campaign against the Creeks. He lived to be 102 years old.

Ophelia Crowder was born November 10, 1895, in the Choctaw Nation near Hugo. Almost a teenager at statehood, her allotment was near Soper. She married Jay Birchfield, whose father, a Hugo blacksmith, had been one of the ones to donate land for the town of Hugo. They moved upriver on the Muddy Boggy to spend the greater portion of their lives near the community of Farris, where her husband dug a spring on Sandy Creek and placed a concrete collar in it, which is still in public use today. They raised a large family, and most of their children raised large families, and their grandchildren and great-grandchildren and great-great-grandchildren are today raising families.

Preceding her in death were: her father, Martin B. Crowder, who died in 1969 at the age of 98; all of her siblings and almost all of her generation of friends and relatives; her husband, who died in 1960; most of her children (John, Elmer, Eula Nowlin, Lee, Edgar and several infants); and a number of her grandchildren and great-grandchildren.

She is survived by her daughter, Alene Prater of Crystal, in whose home she lived for some time preceding her death, and by her two youngest sons, James (Hop) of Oklahoma City, and Bunnie of Farris. Her youngest son was a member of the Choctaw Tribal Council at the time the present Constitution of the Choctaw Nation of Oklahoma was adopted.

Known throughout her life as "Rookie," she was known to most of her descendants simply as "Granny," a diminutive, white-haired bundle of energy who would enthusiastically enter into a game of ball with the children, and who loved to spend an entire day along Sandy Creek catching perch for trot line bait, squealing with delight every time she caught one. She was a joy to be around, full of good cheer, a friend and playmate to each new child in the family. Good-bye, Granny, we miss you very much.

▼

Trip Diary
Thursday, June 11, 1987
61st day in camp
    . . . 7:50 P.M., hurry down the steep riverbank to Boggy, set 2nd trotline in same big hole of water where caught the 7 lb flathead catfish this morning . . . Bait out both lines with live perch from the pond . . . Get half a dozen onions and a few radishes from garden on way back . . . get back to camp just at dark. Light lantern, stove. Make coffee, put catfish on to fry, two big skillets. Tune in halftime of Celtics/Lakers NBA playoff game with Celtics holding big lead. Wash feet. Mosquitos bad in lean-to. Light sprinkles outside when stepped outside the lean-to to wash pan . . . Eat supper, fried catfish, fresh onions, radishes, coffee, Kool Aid, mosquitos. Read paper, swat mosquitos. Light rain at 1 A.M. Kitty comes climbing into lean-to, damp from the rain after eating the big piece of catfish backbone I gave her for her supper. She lays on table in front of me and begins to lick herself dry. Sure is a good cat. My spirits still buoyed over catching 7 lb. flathead this morning. Feel

good about both trotlines set in the big hole of water at the foot of the trail. Would like to add a couple throwlines off rock pile, but doubt that the perch fishing in the pond will consistently be as good as today. Also want to pick enough blackberries tomorrow to make another stove top cobbler. Tune in Louisiana radio station, Cajun fiddling, about 1:25 A.M. (Alton Roget and the Lafayette Playboys). Get pups and go to bed in trailer to get away from mosquitos about 1:30 A.M.

▼

Trip Diary
Friday, June 12, 1987
62nd day in camp

Up 5:45 A.M., make coffee, walk down to river to run the trotlines at 6:30 A.M. Catch one 15 1/2 pound flathead catfish on third hook from snag on far side of river, next to the weight, on the trotline that I set out last night . . . He didn't pull until I turned the boat over on the riverbank to dump out the rainwater. He pulled strong when I got to the line. He was hooked good at corner of mouth. Fought pretty hard getting him in the boat. I thought he was only 8–10 lb. in the boat, 10–12 lb. after carrying him up the hill. He tipped the scales at a solid 15 1/2 lb., nearly a twin to the one Bun and I caught upriver a few weeks ago. Put him in the old bathtub out in the pasture, haul 30 gallons of pond water for the tub. Make coffee. Boggy held steady last night, not rising, so if it rained upriver the water hasn't had time to get here yet . . . Weather cloudy, mildly humid, no breeze, looks like it could rain again. Build fire in firepit, put on pot of beans . . . Dig worms, go to pond, catch a dozen perch. Back to camp off and on to add water to beans and at noon for lunch . . . Take the flathead out of the bathtub and put him in live box in Boggy. He seems in good shape. Set out 3rd trotline in downstream end of big hole of water . . . Water not as deep as I'd hoped, about 6 feet most of the way across. Too much brush in deeper water . . . Also dug out the spring where it had sanded in. Return to camp 2:15 P.M. Coffee break. Bright sunshine now. Moved flathead from bathtub to Boggy because Bun might not make it down to see him today . . . In Boggy live box he might live a few days. Still have fried catfish from 7 pounder fried last night so don't need to clean him now. Walk to the big blackberry thicket south of camp and pick enough blackberries for a cobbler . . . Catch 15 more perch . . . until lightning sets in from the west. Hurry to Boggy with bait at 5:30 P.M. . . . Fresh bait in very good, frisky shape . . . Checked 15 1/2 lb. flathead in live box. OK. Get back to camp at 6 P.M. just as light rain begins to fall . . . Peel and fry taters, make coffee . . . eat quick first install-ment on supper, catfish, taters, onions, radishes, coffee, mosquitos. Head for pond at 7:30 P.M . . . kill water moc-casin with shotgun, he was curled up under the handle of my perch pole. Catch 3 perch before wind squall and bad cloud move in. Hurry to camp. Refuel stove and lantern . . . Set storm flaps . . . Take stand-up bath out in the pasture beside bathtub . . . Kitty wanted outside just before dark, as she usually does. About 9:30 P.M. put on blackberries, sugar (2 cups), water (well covered), let boil awhile. Put new battery in radio temporarily so can hear ballgame without holding radio to ear. Texas Rangers getting pasted at home, 6–1 in 6th inning. Contemplate satisfactions re-garding this morning's catch of 15 1/2 pound flathead: 1) Caught him on a big perch from the pond. Both Uncle Bun and Uncle Hodge dislike big pond perch for trotline bait, mostly because they're not as hardy as the small creek perch out of Sandy and don't live as long on the trotline. But that's what is easiest to catch and most abundant in the pond, big eating-size perch, and that's what I caught the flathead on. The flathead's mouth was lots bigger than the big perch. Easy to see why Great-Uncle Bunnie preferred 2–3 lb. bullhead catfish for bait. It's a hassle walking all the way to Sandy Creek and back to catch small and medium size perch, so if the big catfish will hit the big perch from the pond, it makes it so much easier all the way around to get bait, and can fish longer without getting so worn out; 2) Caught him on the new trotline Dad made before he died and never got to use, making sets that Dad and Uncle Bun taught me how to make. After all the frustrations that Dad and I suffered fishing together for about thirty years trying to catch a catfish out of Boggy bigger than a ten pounder, it feels doubly good to finally have caught one; 3) Caught him the second night after deciding to strike out trotline fishing on my own, and the very next night after catching the 7 pounder and deciding to get serious about fishing the big hole of water at the foot of the trail. In April and May I didn't trust the river not to get up quickly over the lines and wash them away, so was content to fish with throw-lines in the shoals or with trotlines upriver with Uncle Bun. But now am eager to keep trying trotlines in the big hole of water at the foot of the trail; 4) Didn't have to pad-dle way upriver to the old family fishing holes to get him; 5) Everything went right, from catching enough perch to set out the new trotline, to getting to the river early enough, just barely, to get it set out before dark, to getting it strung out without any problems, to getting up early enough to get him off before he twisted off, to the thrill of seeing the snag the line was tied to whipping up and down in the water, to feeling the power of him as he pulled on the line, to landing him in the boat cleanly, to seeing him weigh in at more than I thought he would, and at slightly more than the one Bun and I caught upriver a few weeks ago. Can't wait to see Bun's reaction when he sees the fish. Hope he stays alive in the live box until Bun gets back down. About 10 P.M. make dumplings to go in blackber-ries. Added more sugar and water because last batch was a little dry and not quite sweet enough. Made 4 cups of dumpling mix last time, this time made only 3 cups of mix. Drop in about 2 dozen big dumplings at 10:30 P.M. Ready in 15 minutes. Try cobbler when done. Pretty good. Big full moon tonight. Rangers lose game 6–1. Change back to old battery in radio. Feed pups 2–3 pieces of catfish, picking the meat off the bones for them. Barking Puppy barks all the way through dinner, everytime I give her a piece of fish, and again as soon as she swallows it, guess she was ready to eat some catfish. Go to bed with the pups, in trailer, about 11:30 P.M.

▼

Trip Diary
Saturday, June 13, 1987
63rd day in camp

Up about 8 A.M. Cobbler, coffee for breakfast. Slept like a rock. Run the trotlines . . . The 15 1/2 pound flathead pushed through the bars on the live box and got back in Boggy. Stout, medal rods, but he spread them as wide as his head. Ain't that a kick in the pants . . .

▼

Grannie Birchfield   Monday, June 15, 1987
2540 S.W. 31
Okla City OK

Dear Grannie B.

How do old woman!

It sure is hot down here. I'll bet it's hot up there, too. Well this Boggy Bottom boy has been lipping the catfish. Last Thursday morning I caught a 7 pound Flathead. Friday morning I caught a 15 1/2 pound Flathead. Sunday morning I caught a 8 1/2 pound Blue. This morning I caught a 2 pound Flathead.

The blackberries are everywhere. I made a stove top blackberry cobbler with dumplings. It sure was good.

The Blue catfish sure did taste good. But the 15 1/2 pound Flathead was the best storyteller. Nobody can tell a good story like a big Flathead.

I didn't know anything about how they tell stories until I was getting ready to clean him. I was sharpening my knife with him hanging from the tree flopping around. He said, "What are you doing?"

I said, "I'm getting ready to clean you and eat you."

He said, Well that was only fair being as how I had caught him. Then he said he remembered me. Wasn't I the old boy that came down here summer before last fishing in the shoals?

I said that was me allright.

He said he was just a little 5 pounder then and liked to play in the shoals. He said he remembered one night when he swam up the shoals and stole everyone of my baits off my throwlines.

I said, "Why you rascal. I'm going to clean you and eat you for that."

He said, "You're going to clean me and eat me, anyway."

I said that was true.

He said, "I'll tell you what. If you'll let me down from hanging from this tree and take me down to the creek and let me spend the night in the live box down there so I can have one last night in Boggy, then tomorrow morning I'll tell you how I stole all your baits summer before last."

I said I sure would like to know how he stole all those baits. And I guessed I had plenty of catfish to eat that day. So I took him down from the tree and carried him down to Boggy and put him in the live box. I tied down the lid double good all around and tied a big, long stout rope to the live box and threw it out in the creek.

The next morning when I went down to get him that rascal had pushed his head through the wires in the cage and got away. Now here I am, I still don't know how he stole all those baits summer before last.

I'll tell you what. Those big Flatheads are pretty to look at and good to eat. But the next one that starts telling me a story, I'm not going to pay any attention to anything he says.

Well, it's about time for me to go catch some more perch in the pond. I now have a kitty cat down here. A

wild mammy cat moved in with me and the puppies. She is a good mouse catcher.
Take care,
Love, Don

▼

Trip Diary
Wednesday, April 26, 1989
117th day in camp

Up 7 A.M., beautiful morning, birds singing, Dallas radio temp 70 degrees. 7:35 A.M., leave to run the four trotlines far upriver. Return 8:45 A.M., all excited. Caught nothing on first line. Caught a 5 lb. humpback blue catfish on second line, near where Grandpa had his boat landing at great-grandfather Crowder's old corn field. Paddled up the shoals feeling pretty good. Caught a 2 lb. channel catfish on the third line, just above the shoals. And, in the same big hole of water where Uncle Hodge caught the twin 34 pounders at each end of a trotline about forty or fifty years ago, in the very swift water right in the narrows at the head of the big hole of water, caught a 34 lb. flathead catfish on the fourth line. He was pulling very hard, on the 4th hook from the far side. He had swallowed about 2/3rds of a 4 lb. blue catfish that I'd caught on the line sometime during the night, pulled the hook loose from the blue, and got himself hooked very good deep in the bottom of his mouth. He had been pulling so hard that he had broken the limb in half that the line was tied to, giving him some slack in the line to work with. What a time getting him into the boat. In the swift water he nearly took me into the river with him. With the river so low and clear, as low and clear as in August, I could see him flashing back and forth at terrific speed when I was almost on top of him, incredible bursts of frenzied energy. I swear, in the boat he looked nearly as big as the 65 pounder Uncle Hodge caught last week, but not nearly as fat. Paddle back to camp in record time, literally sailing down through the shoals. Tie the catfish to the boat through the mouth and gills. Put the 5 lb. blue and 2 lb. channel cat in with the 7 lb flathead in the live box in the pond. Change into a pair of pants that doesn't have the crotch ripped out. Fire the gun so the crazy hound dog that adopted me will run off and hide, which she does. Walk out of the bottom to the nearest neighbor's house, call Uncle Bun's, tell Aunt Bea to tell him I caught a good one . . . Am down at the boat looking at the fish when they arrive with a set of bathroom scales . . . Bun hefts him and guesses him at 38 lbs . . . he weighs 34 . . . I take the scales into the old, off-loaded camper and weigh myself naked, which is how I weighted when I left the city this time. I now weigh 175 lbs, down 25 lbs from the even 200 lbs that I weighed New Year's Eve when I left Oklahoma City . . . I begin cleaning the 7 pounder from the live box on the pond . . . Uncle Hodge arrives as Bun starts to clean the 34 pounder . . . Hodge hefts him and also guesses him at 38 lbs. Bun says his scales surely must be off about four pounds. We all sit around and visit awhile after cleaning the fish. I give them half the fish, plus the backbones. Bun cuts my half into 51 pieces for frying . . . it makes 8 skillets of catfish, two complete fryings, using all four big skillets. Then put on two skillets of big thick pieces for the crazy hound dog (the 7 lb. flathead and the 4 lb blue that the 34 pounder was trying to swallow.) . . . More relatives arrive . . . We talk about all the big fish that my kinfolks have caught out of Boggy down through the years, the biggest being the 76 pound flathead that Uncle Bun and Uncle Edgar caught when I was a kid. They talk especially about the 40 pounder Uncle Elmer caught which had nearly swallowed about a 4 pounder on the trotline, just like mine tried to do, and they laugh so hard they nearly cry, trying to mimic Uncle Elmer's deep, gravely voice when he raised the line and the fish came floating up to the surface, "Goddamn, Pa, this one's got a tail at both ends."

Part IV

▼ ▼ ▼ ▼ ▼ ▼ ▼ ▼ ▼

The Case Against History
▼▼▼▼▼▼▼▼▼▼▼▼▼▼▼▼

Indians know that stories are more reliable guides to a people and their past than works of history. Many of us who have received formal training in how to follow the often subtle rules for determining what sort of evidence may be deemed reliable, and thus admissible, in this alien, European art form called history have come to love it as a discipline. We have also learned to distrust it.

It cannot tell the truth. Historians rely most heavily upon written evidence, letters, diaries, reports. Whatever goes unrecorded is not likely to find its way into "history." Worse yet, when a Native people and a European people first come into contact, the admissible historical evidence is mostly one-sided. Story, however, is oral tradition. Of course, whatever is left unsaid between the generations gets lost. However, a great deal less, of actual value, gets lost in the oral tradition than in "history." A people's stories about themselves, their world, and their past may leave many things unsaid, but on the whole, the things that do get said, and the way they are said, give a clearer picture of that people than any work of history can ever give.

History is a foreign academic discipline, one invented by the ancient Greeks. Its power was first appreciated by Herodotus and was then demonstrated magnificently by Thucydides. To understand how foolish this ancient Greek invention actually is, it is only necessary to take a look at the people who have been promoting it lately. In the twentieth century, the two biggest promoters of Herodotus and Thucydides have been Robert Maynard Hutchins and Mortimer J. Adler. Hutchins, as editor in chief, and Adler, as associate editor, of the Encyclopeadia Britannica *Great Books of the Western World*, brought us volume 6 of that series, *Herodotus/Thucydides* in 1952.

And who are Robert Maynard Hutchins and Mortimer J. Adler? These are the two clowns who abolished college football at the University of Chicago on December 23, 1939. At that time Hutchins was president of the University of Chicago, and his sidekick Adler, his trusted confidant, was an associate professor.

Why these two abolished football when they got control of the University of Chicago has always been a head scratcher. Both of them were deeply imbued in ancient Greek life, and love of vigorous athleticism is at the very core of ancient Greek culture. Hutchins (who died in 1977) was a serious student of Thomas Aquinas, who was himself a great exponent of Aristotle, and Adler is universally regarded as the greatest modern exponent of Aristotle.

We may never know why Hutchins failed to appreciate the ancient Greek love of athleticism, but we can thank Bill Moyers of public television for some hint of why Adler failed to appreciate it. In a television interview with Adler some years ago, Moyers coaxed Adler into admitting that he had failed to receive his bachelor's degree at Columbia University because he personally hated physical exertion so much that he refused to take the compulsory swimming test, which was a requirement for the B.A. degree at Columbia at that time.

It might also be noted here that there are good reasons why anyone should be skeptical of Aristotle and of anyone imbued with his teachings. If Aristotle stood for anything in the art of politics, surely it was for the principle that a ruler should rule by moderation. Regarding these ancient Greeks and their philosophers, bear in mind that Aristotle had been a student of Plato, and that Plato had been a student of Socrates, and that Aristotle, himself, became the personal tutor of Alexander the Great. Aristotle was such a good teacher of moderation that his prize pupil went out and tried to conquer the whole known world.

Fans of the University of Oklahoma Sooner football team might well scratch their heads concerning another aspect of college football having been abolished at Chicago by Hutchins and Adler. The Chicago University football coach who lost his job in 1939 when the program got the ax was none other than Clark Daniel Shaughnessy, who had one of the most miserable records in all of college football, having lost more than twice as many games as he'd won in his six years at Chicago. Nevertheless, Shaughnessy was immediately called to Stanford, where the college president, Ray Lyman Wilbur, thought that Shaughnessy had invented the T-formation.

Wilbur had seen pro football's Chicago Bears use the T-formation to slaughter the Washington Redskins 73–0 and was certain that Shaughnessy was the man to run the Stanford Indians' football team. Shaughnessy, never slow on the uptake, and fresh from one encounter with a college president who didn't know the difference between a football and a box of rocks, listened to Wilbur's bubbling pride at having hired away "Chicago's T-formation man" and stunned the college football world by announcing that Stanford would switch to the T, which was considered much too complex for college ball, especially for the Stanford team, which hadn't even scored ten touchdowns the previous year using the fairly simple single-wing formation and which had gained a reputation as the free spirits of the college football world, more proficient at clearing out roadside taverns than anything else.

Improvising the pro T to suit his talent, especially the considerable talents of a Bronko Nagurski clone at fullback named Norm Standlee, and introducing intricate, concentrated chalk talks elaborating line blocking schemes for sixty new plays, shuttling tackles and ends, shifting guards, employing brand new schemes which featured a flanker and a man in motion away from the play, and moving a mediocre single-wing tailback named Frankie Albert, who had great faking ability, to quarterback, Shaughnessy's 1940 Stanford Indians beat San Francisco 27–0, Oregon 13–0, Santa Clara 7–6, Washington State 26–14, Southern Cal 21–7, UCLA 20–14, Washington 20–10, Oregon State 28–14, California 13–7, and then beat Nebraska 21–13 in the 1941 Rose Bowl. It was the greatest Indians team that Stanford ever fielded and one of the best that college football has ever seen.

All the way across the continent, a young Jim Tatum, fresh from a three-year stint as varsity baseball coach at Cornell, who was an assistant football coach under Bear Wolf at the University of North Carolina in 1940, and whose primary duty was scouting future opponents, took notice of what Shaughnessy was doing with the Indians' offense. So did a young part-time backfield coach named Charles "Bud" Wilkinson, who was pursuing a master's degree at the University of Syracuse, and who in 1938 had been named the scholar-athlete of the Big Ten Conference, and who had then quarterbacked the College All-Stars to their first victory over the pros, beating the Green Bay Packers, 6–0.

But the man who was most intrigued by what Shaughnessy was doing with the Indians in 1940 was the seasoned coach of the University of Missouri, Don Faurot, who immediately began tinkering even further with Shaughnessy's innovations, discovering an entire world that began opening up for a team whose quarterback operated parallel to the line of scrimmage, inventing what would soon become known as the Split-T formation. When World War II and the United States Navy brought Faurot, Tatum, and Wilkinson together at Iowa Navy Pre-Flight School, the nearly limitless possibilities of the Split-T formation dominated their conversations.

In 1946, with the war over, Tatum became head coach at Oklahoma, taking Wilkinson with him as an assistant, where they immediately installed the Split-T. The next year, after Tatum moved to Maryland, Wilkinson became head coach of the Sooners and used the Split-T to kick the most serious butt in the history of college football, reeling off thirty-one consecutive victories in one stretch, and then topping that by racking up the untouchable record of forty-seven straight, leaving us to wonder whether we should love Adler and Hutchins for abolishing college football at Chicago, without which the Split-T formation might never have been invented, and the Sooners might not have won national championships in 1950, 1955, and 1956, or whether we should be suspicious not only of Adler and Hutchins, but of anyone they might have ever talked to, and of any children they might have ever had, and of anyone who might have ever read any of their books, for fear that the impulse that led them to start abolishing college football programs might be contagious, or capable of being transmitted subliminally through their writings, or might be something that gets handed down in their genes.

With men like that promoting Herodotus and Thucydides and the discipline of history, can there be any doubt that the case against history is a strong one?

(see *Football's Greatest Coaches* by Edwin Pope (Atlanta: Tupper and Love, Inc., 1955), "Donald Burrows Faurot, Originator of the Split-T," pps. 96–104, "Clark Daniel Shaughnessy, Daddy of the Modern T," pps. 219–230, "James Moore Tatum, Silent Jim? Well, Not Actually," pps. 258–268, and "Charles (Bud) Wilkinson, Run! Run! Run!," pps. 303–310; see also "A Conversation with Mortimer J. Adler: The designer of the Syntopicon talks with Bill Moyers," 58 minutes, AUDIO-TEXT Cassettes #38820, from: The Center for Cassette Studies, Inc., 8110 Webb Ave., N. Hollywood, CA 91605).

Dedicatory Poetry
And Dedicatory Poets:
The Laughing Boy, The Braying Laughter,
And The Blithe Spirit

A young Oliver La Farge, in the 1920s, did not know that the novel he was writing would win the Pulitzer Prize for literature. He was merely following a compulsion to record some of the many impressions he had received during his years among the Navajos in the southwest.

It was a good time to write a novel about the Navajos. It was before the automobile changed the face of the southwest forever, bringing great distances within reach, bringing even the southwest itself within easy reach of anyone, anywhere. It was before television, before World War II, before the Great Depression, before rural electrification. It was a different world. It was still the time of the horse, and horse racing, and horse race romances.

It was the time of *Laughing Boy*, who, with a carefree, reckless indifference could happily wager all of his possessions, even his pony, on the sure-footed speed of his pony.

When Oliver La Farge had finished his novel and sat down to pen a dedicatory poem for it, he brought to the poem some of that same carefree, reckless spirit.

Dedicated
to
the only beautiful squaw I have ever seen
in all my life, whose name I have forgotten

This dedication has always seemed a bit ambiguous. Does it mean that the poet has only seen one beautiful Indian woman in all his life? As a matter of grammar the placement of the comma would seem to give it this meaning, a sort of "I have been among their women, and they are ugly."

Or does it mean that he has seen many beautiful Indian women and can remember all of their names, but one, and it is that one to whom the book is dedicated? "Squaw," one might note, is a term not much used by Indians.

The extent to which Indian women were puzzled by the delicacies and nuances regarding this fine point of English grammar, and the persistence with which they sought clarification from the author on this matter, might be inferred by noting that, more than three decades after the novel first appeared, upon the occasion of being asked to write an introduction to a new printing of his novel in 1962, Oliver La Farge, by then a much older and wiser man, recanted his dedicatory poem and confided that it had been a matter of deep embarrassment to him and one he wished he had never written. Perhaps the Navajo women had been hounding him unmercifully.

Not all books, of course, or even very many books, have dedicatory poems, and of those which do, not all authors write their own poetry. When Rennard Strickland published *The Indians In Oklahoma*, in 1981, he chose for a dedication a passage from *Wah Kon-Tah* by John Joseph Mathews, the great chronicler of the Osages—The Children of the Middle Waters.

> Where the Indian passed in dignity, disturbing nothing and leaving Nature as he had found her; with nothing to record his passage, except a footprint or a broken twig, the white man plundered and wasted and shouted; frightening the silences with his great braying laughter and his cursing

This passage by Mathews is particularly well suited as a dedication to Strickland's book, a book that narrates the Indians' struggle to maintain their cultural identity and give voice to the uniqueness of each tribe's cultural heritage amid the din of the great braying laughter.

Strickland (an Osage/Cherokee) knows that "there has never been a single, unified Oklahoma Indian culture," (7) and his book is rich with examples of the wide diversity among Native peoples in Oklahoma. He openly challenges the white man's concept of "progress" and argues that the Indian's ability to admit that he cannot win an unlimited war against nature is more rational than the theory of progress, as well as being a central thread that ties many otherwise diverse Indian cultures together. After publishing *The Indians In Oklahoma*, Strickland became Professor of Law and Director of the Center for the Study of American Indian Law and Policy at the University of Oklahoma College of Law, and he is now Dean of the University of Oregon Law School.

Sometimes a dedicatory poem will offer an opportunity for an author to share some deeply felt emotion. Such was the case in 1971 when the late Arrell M. Gibson published his history of a Native people, simply entitled *The Chickasaws*.

Dedicatory
Sam Gibson
Brother mine and mankind
Artist, raconteur
Blithe spirit and simple trust
Living in a rush
Missing naught, tasting all
Strong in Life, bravest at Death's door
His legacy—paintings, humor, kindness, serenity

It is fitting for Native people to share the sense of personal loss of an author who labored so long in their behalf. Arrell M. Gibson, "Gib" to all who knew him, wrote many works of history of interest to Indians, among them *The Kickapoos—Lords of the Middle Border.*

A research professor of history for many years in the University of Oklahoma, he was chairman of the history department when I wandered into his office more than a quarter of a century ago to see about pursuing graduate studies, three weeks after classes had started, without any transcripts, without having taken the Graduate Records Examination, without having made application for admission, without having done anything except show up at his office, without an appointment. Though he was among the busiest people in Oklahoma he took time out to get me into school.

Stories about Gibson are now legend on the OU campus, many of them about how he juggled his unbelievably busy schedule. He was director of so many institutions (the Stovall Museum and the Western History Collections and the Manuscript Division of the University of Oklahoma among them), and he was on the boards of directors of so many others, that the more one knows about the man the more one stands in awe of his incredible energies. He had five different offices at OU when I first met him, and he was rumored to have another one of which only he knew the location.

For all of his achievements, Gib was a modest, quiet, self-effacing man, happiest when deep in the midst of his research. There is a story told about him that illustrates his sense of humor.

It seems that some years ago he was invited to return to a small college in the Ozarks to receive that college's honor as one of its outstanding alumni. After a busy weekend of banquets and speeches, he took a solitary Saturday night stroll down the town's main street to absorb once again the sights and sounds of his youth. Outside an old pool hall lounged one of the town's old timers, who recognized Gib as the boy known as "Lukie" from many years earlier, a boy who had been quite good at the pool table.

"What are you doing these days?" asked the old timer, who obviously didn't know why Gibson was in town.

"Well," said Gib, looking down at the ground and shuffling his feet, "I'm a professional gambler over in Oklahoma."

"That a boy, Lukie!" said the old timer, slapping Gib on the back. "I always knew you'd make good."

Steve Frazee and Me

▼ ▼ ▼ ▼ ▼ ▼ ▼ ▼ ▼ ▼ ▼ ▼ ▼ ▼ ▼ ▼

Mick Jagger is drowning out the crickets, telling about how he can't get no satisfaction. The radio is louder than usual, coming from a cabin down the hill, because tonight there is a festive, anticipatory air throughout Bo Belcher's Chandler Oklahoma Baseball Camp.

Tomorrow a professional baseball scout will be here to look us over. Moose, the seventeen year-old who can park 'em over the center field fence, might get a contract offer. That has everyone excited. Everyone likes Moose.

Today the old man himself talked to us. Bo Belcher had been around baseball a long time and knew a lot of stories. He told us one that prepared us, in his way, for tomorrow. He told about the kid the scout didn't bother talking to, a kid who might have been able to pitch, because the scout saw the kid with his cap on backwards, awkwardly trying to pitch with his left hand, just for fun.

"I'm only interested in men who take baseball seriously," said the scout to Mr. Belcher, despite Belcher's pleas to watch him throw a few.

"The kid is good," said Belcher, to no avail.

We had all night to think about that story, and the next day nobody, certainly not fifteen year-old me, not even any of the peewees, had his cap on backwards.

Moose did pretty good in the demo game against a team from an Oklahoma City suburb, a pretty salty bunch. He went three for four against their ace, parking one. The fourth one was a loud foul just within reach of the left fielder at the bleachers. The other two were doubles. Damn were we proud of him.

He didn't get a contract offer.

▼

That Christmas I was coming off the crutches, coming out of the cast. My whole world fell apart on one kickoff return on a sandlot football field three weeks before varsity football practice started at the beginning of my high school career. The break was a bad one. Coming out of the cast I barely recognized my right leg, it was so withered away, so ugly yellow, so scrawny. It would take all the rest of high school to rehabilitate it.

Something snapped, something other than the leg bone. The difference between my high school years and my years in junior high school would be as though two different people had come along who shared nothing in common but the same name. If I wasn't going to be a world class athlete, by God, I wasn't going to be anything.

I quit everything. I quit violin. I'd carried one since the fourth grade, but no more, not with the damn crutches. I quit drama. I never stepped on a stage in a theatrical role again. I quit gymnastics, having been one of the few to earn a letter in the ninth grade.

I gave up biology and all other laboratory sciences. That didn't have anything to do with the broken leg. It had to do with one of the more popular girls in school collapsing one day in lab and dying, right there on the floor in front of us all, from a burst blood vessel in her brain. I steered clear of the lab sciences after that. I couldn't look at a room filled with microscopes without remembering how her eyes rolled up, and how she slobbered, and did other things that shouldn't happen to a pretty girl in public.

I gave no more morning prayer devotionals over the intercom. I was master of ceremonies of no more Oklahoma City educational television orchestra productions, played no more public performances in a string quartet, played no more second violin in the Oklahoma City Junior Symphony, never again went deep in the hole at short stop to snag it backhanded, transfer the ball, plant the foot, leap high in the air, and nail the runner at first base, took no more opportunities to stand before the assembled student body to debate who should be elected President of the United States, and, for good measure, never again set foot in a church, except for a wedding or a funeral, breaking a five-year perfect attendance record in Sunday School.

I was pissed.

▼

I was already disgusted with what I had learned about the Choctaws. I'd been intensely proud of my Choctaw blood, from my father's side of the family, until I read Anna Lewis' *Chief Pushmataha, American Patriot: The Story of the Choctaws Struggle for Survival* and Angie Debo's *Rise and Fall of the Choctaw Republic*. When I learned how the United States had betrayed the Choctaws, the most loyal allies the United States ever had, I could not comprehend why the Choctaws did not fight back, even if it meant getting annihilated. Honor demanded nothing less, but they didn't do it. Instead, they allowed the United States Army to march them all the way from Mississippi to where I had been born.

It would change the way I looked at the United States. After that I would begin to see through the propaganda, the self-delusion, and the ethnocentricity of American historians. While others around me were absorbing the American version of American history, mostly with impatience and indifference, I was alive to it, but it was an interest born of distrust and skepticism. It was nothing, however, compared to my disgust with the Choctaws, for allowing the United States to get away with what it had done to them.

I thought my father was a colossal fool, because he had gotten religion in a big way and was now doing the work of the proselytizing, fundamentalist Christians, the one group, I was beginning to realize, who had done more to destroy Indian cultures, languages, and religions than all the land speculators, politicians, and soldiers put together. I blamed my mother for making a fool out of Dad, and me. She was the one who had gotten us all involved in the church, when I was ten years old. Before that, all Dad had cared about was hunting and fishing. I decided that Dad would have been a lot better off if he had never gotten married. They tried to put their foot down when I quit the church, but the cussing I gave them put them both in a state of shock.

I was mad at the world and at everybody in it.

▼

I withdrew almost completely into the world of juvenile outdoor fiction. Those books spoke to me. My Choctaw great-grandfather and great-uncle lived at the end of the road, at the western edge of the Ouachita Mountains in southeastern Oklahoma, where I had been born, and where we lived until we moved to the city when I was four years old. For the next six years, until we joined the church, we went back home almost every weekend. Both sets of grandparents still lived down there, along with most of my aunts and uncles and cousins. There weren't many roads, there weren't many people, and it seemed almost a wilderness.

I had grown up knowing two different worlds, the suburbs of Oklahoma City, where practically everything was brand new, and the backwoods of southeastern Oklahoma, where some of my Choctaw relatives still cooked on woodburning stoves, hauled water from a spring on a horsedrawn sled, and didn't own cars or even know how to drive. They practically lived outdoors, and about all they ever did was hunt and fish. It was the closest thing to paradise I had ever known. It might have been the 1950s in the suburbs of Oklahoma City, but in the backwoods of southeastern Oklahoma it was still the nineteenth century.

When I read Jim Kjelgaard or Stephen W. Meader, or Lew Dietz, or any of the other writers of outdoor juvenile fiction, I wasn't reading fiction, I was reading about a world I knew.

I spent a lot of time roaming that world in fantasy, planning what I would do when I got out of school. I'd have a good pair of boots and a backpack, and there wouldn't be anything to keep me from wandering free, living off the land.

▼

When it became clear that I was not going to rejoin the human race, Dad enlisted the help of the most knowledgeable person he knew, a man named Slagle. Mr. Slagle and his wife had both retired from careers with the International Red Cross. They'd long since raised their family, and their kids were all dentists and school superintendents and things like that. Mr. Slagle had played semi-pro baseball. He was also a skilled outdoorsman. We started fishing together.

One day Mr. Slagle took me into his library. He was a dedicated reader of Westerns, and the room was filled with them, on every shelf, wall to wall. He handed one to me, saying, "I think you might like this one."

It was *Many Rivers To Cross*, by Steve Frazee, published in 1955. I didn't know it at the time, but that was the year Frazee had been elected the third president of Western Writers of America. Never in my life had I read a book that spoke to me so directly. Its hero was a man who cared about nothing but the good life, roaming wild and free on the Kentucky frontier.

Except for some continually recurring nonsense about a good looking girl out to trap him into marriage, and a ridiculous ending where she finally nailed his butt, the book articulated a philosophy of life so close to mine that it was almost as though someone had read my mind. For one thing, the hero was dead set against the institution of marriage, and for all the reasons that had already occurred to me, plus some that I hadn't even thought of yet. I had to read the book two or three times just trying to figure out where the hero had gone wrong, and I finally decided that Frazee must have written it that way as a cautionary tale to show all that could go wrong if a man wasn't careful, and to show a whole lot of things that could go wrong even if he was careful.

It was the first time it had ever occurred to me that books might be written in different ways. It also occurred to me that I might write a book some day, and if I did, I'd write one a whole lot like that book, but not give it such a tragic ending.

The truly great thing about the book was its humor. The hero was a white guy who had been captured by Shawnees as a kid and raised as a Shawnee. He had tried to reenter the white world, but he was really out of place in both worlds. At that time, anything having to do with Indians was a real sore spot with me, and I had never imagined that it might be possible to laugh about it. But this book was funny. It helped me to learn how to laugh about some of the more ridiculous features of my own situation, torn between the two branches of my heritage.

It also woke me up in a big way that I'd better be darn careful around girls, or I might end up getting nailed just like the hero in that book. I was able to see how it might be possible to be philosophically opposed to marriage and still end up getting nailed. I began to realize that the next few years were going to be critical for me if I were going to preserve my personal freedom, and who was I to be brooding about things like history or lost athletic opportunities when any minute one of those scheming females might decide to spring a trap.

I started searching for and collecting Frazee's books. There was nothing quite like the thrill of finding one I didn't have. His pulp Westerns, the paperback originals from the 1950s, started getting harder to find in used book stores during the 1970s. Nowadays about the only ones you ever see are the two that have been continuously reprinted, *Many Rivers To Cross* and *He Rode Alone*. I continued to collect his work for many years, until, after looking for it for about twenty years, I finally found a first printing of *Many Rivers To Cross* (.25 cover price, with original cover art, in fair condition). By then I had dozens of copies of that book, reflecting all the changes in cover art or cover price (at one time I'd had close to a hundred copies, but I'd given away most of them).

I also eventually found multiple copies of *He Rode Alone*, *The Sky Block*, *A Gun For Bragg's Woman*, *Flight 409*, *The Outcasts*, *Lawman's Feud*, *Desert Guns*, *Cry Coyote*, *The Gun Throwers*, *The Way Through The Mountains*, *Fire In The Valley*, *Smoke In The Valley*, *A Day To Die*, *Rendezvous*, *Running Target*, *The Alamo*, *Gold At Kansas Gulch*, and single copies of *Tumbling Range Woman*, *Gunman's Land*, *High Hell*, *More Damn Tourists*, a couple of his Lassie titles, and *We Only Kill Each Other* (under the pen name Dean Jennings). I also found some of his short stories in anthologies. I looked for 1953 issues of *Argosy* magazine, where an early version of *Many Rivers To Cross* had originally appeared as a short story, but I never found it.

▼

It was not long after Mr. Slagle gave me that first copy of *Many River To Cross* that Dad took me to work with him one day at the steel company where he worked for thirteen years. It was an eye-opener, all the grime, the noise, the dust. Dad told me that this was the kind of life I was heading toward if I didn't straighten up and take an interest in things like trying to get an education. I decided, on the spot, that I would be a writer.

I didn't think I could ever be a kind of writer like Frazee or any of the other authors I liked, but I though I might be able to learn how to be an outdoor magazine writer, where photos were an important part of the articles.

I knew I had a lot of problems if I were going to try to be a writer. For one thing, I was terrible at spelling, and English had never been a good subject for me. But I thought I might be able to learn how to take photos, and maybe my writing would improve as time went along. I would travel the land hunting and fishing and writing about it. What a life! Maybe I'd also learn how to write juvenile outdoor fiction.

Throughout the rest of high school I diligently read magazines like *The Writer* and *Writer's Digest*, and I bought *Writer's Market* and ordered sample copies and writer's guidelines from nearly every outdoor magazine that was listed. I joined the old Outdoor Life Book Club and started building a library. I discovered that writers had bio sketches in reference books like *Contemporary Authors*. I looked up the writers who were clearly the leaders in the outdoor field, especially Erwin A. Bauer and Byron W. Dalrymple, and studied their backgrounds. I noticed that both of them had gone to college, which was what really made me decide that I had to go to college too. I also found out that they had pen names, like Ken Bourbon for Bauer, which amazed me because it seemed like Bauer's byline was already in practically every outdoor magazine being published.

I have long thought that the minute I entered college and got absorbed in academics I forgot all about my ambition to be an outdoor writer. But recently I came across an old letter that shows that as late as the spring of my freshman year it was still the foremost thing on my mind.

March 23, 1967
Dear Don:

I bet you don't know who this is that is typing this little note to you? I don't! Anyway, how have things been with you lately? O.K.? Hope so! What have you been doing? By the way, how is the story that you have been working on so hard, coming along? I sure hope that you can sell it! That would be really tough! How much do you think you can sell it for? What magazine are you thinking about offering it to? *Feild and Stream*? I spelled 'Field' wrong, didn't I? Oh, well, that's life. Ha!!!!!

I got home at about 9:45 Wednesday night, and my mother was waiting up for me. You will never guess what she said to me. It real got 'hot'! No, not really, she just asked me where I had been, and I (natuarally) told her that I had been with you. Was *THAT* alright? Hope so, cause that is what I said.

By just reading this little note, do you still want me to type your research papers for you? I have mispelled a few words and typed over one, and who nose (ha-ha-knows) how many more mistakes that I will make before I get little note finished.

Guess I had better go, the bell is going to ring?!!!!!!! Will see you tonite! Okie-Dokie?? By the time you have read this note you will have already seen me!! Big thrill-not really!!!

Your friend and mine (I hope),

Linda

▼

By coincidence I ended up graduating from the same college as Frazee, Western State College of Colorado at Gunnison. It happened because my family moved to western Colorado the night I graduated from high school.

After going to the junior college in Grand Junction (which later became a four-year school), and bouncing around from the University of Colorado and the University of Denver and working in the molybdenum mine at Leadville, I finally landed at Western State College. I'd seen some of the world by then, had toured eight countries in South America on a student fact-finding delegation for People-To-People, had worked for Rockefeller at the Republican National Convention, trying to stop Nixon in 1968, and had been heavy into student politics, having been student body president of the junior college and then president of the Colorado Collegiate Association, an umbrella organization of all the college student governments in Colorado. But I was sick of all of that and just wanted a quiet place to finish college. I was aware, of course, that I was at Frazee's old school.

I had enjoyed some academic success, had won the Hazel Butler Garms U.S. History Award from the Daughters of the American Revolution and the R.C. Walker Award from the Grand Junction *Daily Sentinel*. I'd written a column for the school paper and had published a feature article in *Collegiate Scene Magazine*. I'd traveled throughout the state working with student governments on college campuses, including Western State.

When I enrolled in school at Gunnison I already knew some of the people in the college administration and most of the student leaders. I was asked to do a book review for the local radio station. I chose Frazee's latest novel, *Flight 409*, a modern high mountain adventure yarn about a plane crash and rescue. I'd learned a lot about Frazee's career by then, enough to know that I didn't much care for his politics and didn't like some of his work, but that didn't keep me from being a fan. I learned a lot more about him while preparing to do the radio book review when I interviewed Rial Lake, the long-time publicity director at the college, who was one of Frazee's Western State classmates in the class of '37.

As the years went by I would occasionally see critical comments about Frazee's work, such as in the *Encyclopedia of Frontier and Western Fiction*: "Frazee attempted to give all of his westerns a strong historical flavor, but his weakest area was in his highly romanticized and questionable treatment of Native Americans." I would ponder such statements and be able to see some truth in them.

Maybe he romanticized Indians a bit, like the wise, old Oykywha in *Many Rivers To Cross*, and maybe his villainous "Mingoes" in the same book were stereotypes, caricatures of the real Mingoes, the so-called Senecas of Sandusky; but, on the whole, if critics want to maintain that his Indians behaved in ways for which there isn't an abundance of support in the historical record, they've got their work cut out for them.

I would never become much of a critic of Frazee's work. Some things in life you are just too close to to want to see the blemishes. The things that would give me pause would be his books like *The Sky Block*, with its McCarthy era message that anyone might secretly be a communist; but even there, Frazee's engaging and entertaining fourteen-paragraph recitation of how the Red agent, Okie Saunders, set up shop beside a mountain highway in Colorado is Frazee at the top of his form.

I often thought about writing a fan letter to Frazee, or, when I was in school in Gunnison, maybe even visiting him. He only lived a fairly short distance away, over the divide in Salida. But I never did.

After leaving Colorado, and after a couple of years of graduate study in colonial Latin American history, I was in my second year of law school in 1974 at the University of Oklahoma when I learned that Frazee was going to be honored at homecoming as one of Western State's outstanding alumni. I went back for it. I finally got to meet him. We had a chance to talk for a few minutes.

It didn't take him long to figure out that I was a pretty big fan, and we had a good talk. We talked especially about the humor in *Many Rivers To Cross*, the interplay between the characters. I got to ask him why the misprinted date of 1890 for the book's setting had never been corrected in all the printings the book had gone through, and whether the date was supposed to be 1790, since the book took place on the Kentucky frontier and everyone was carrying muzzleloading rifles. He said yes, the date was supposed to be 1790, but that there was an even bigger error in the book that he wished he could get corrected even more than the date. Before he could explain, we got interrupted and he got whisked away by his family and friends. Wouldn't you know it? Now I'll have that to wonder about for the rest of my life.

▼

It was a sad day for me when I learned that Frazee had written the novelization of the Batjac production of "The Alamo. It nearly killed me when I saw "The Alamo" and heard John Wayne say, "Just speak right up and call me Crockett. Don't bother to use my title. Old drunken General Flatford gave it to me in the Choctaw Indian War."

That's Hollywood for you. Just pick a tribe and make up a war. Whoever heard of Choctaws anyway? Just point the camera at John Wayne and give him something to read.

There has never been any such thing as a "Choctaw Indian War." Choctaws are a people who never shed American blood, who provided scouts for generals Morgan, Wayne, Sullivan, and Washington in the American Revolution, who expelled Tecumseh from their country in November, 1811, when Tecumseh came south to try to recruit the Southern nations, who then worked hard to keep a large portion of the Creeks from joining Tecumseh's confederation, then provided Choctaw warriors under Pushmataha to fight in Andrew Jackson's army against the Red Stick faction of the Creeks in the War of 1812 (the really big, decisive war for Indians, and for the American frontier), who provided Choctaw troops for Jackson against the Seminoles in the Peninsular Campaign, and who provided Choctaw troops for Jackson against the British at the Battle of New Orleans. Their reward was to get driven from their homeland in three brutal winter forced marches that killed 2,500 of them. Then they got their new homeland taken from them, too, by the Dawes Commission and Oklahoma statehood. Then they get mocked by Hollywood.

It was just another day's work for the Duke, on a project that took fourteen years to bring to the silver screen at a cost of twelve million dollars, and which has come to symbolize, for Choctaws, both American ignorance of and indifference to the sacrifices of a forgotten people who cast their lot with the Americans.

Out of a sense of loyalty to a favorite author, I dutifully

collected several copies of *The Alamo.* But I've never read it. I don't want to know if Frezee might have repeated that same careless line of dialogue from the screenplay. I'd rather not know something like that.

We all have heroes, and we don't like to see them tarnished. Frazee spoke to me in an important way, with humor, through the pages of *Many Rivers To Cross*, at a time when I needed that medicine, at a time when it helped to change my life, and for that he will always be one of my heroes.

Slouching Towards Hillerman
▼ ▼ ▼ ▼ ▼ ▼ ▼ ▼ ▼ ▼ ▼ ▼ ▼ ▼ ▼

I open Joan Didion's *Play It As It Lays* and I'm in trouble on the third word: "What makes Iago evil?"

I wonder for a moment if that was one of the stages of development that a moth goes through. It seems the fictional Dr. Hannibal "the cannibal" Lecter had something to say about that in Thomas Harris' *Silence Of The Lambs*. But no, that was an *imago*. A quick check of *Funk & Wagnalls Standard College Dictionary* tells me, sure enough, that an imago is "An insect in its adult, sexually mature stage."

It's funny how you can go your entire life without being aware of such a thing as a moth, and then read a book like *Silence Of The Lambs* and suddenly you see them everywhere, even in Didion, where, so far, they haven't even shown up.

I was reading Tom Robbins' *Another Roadside Attraction* the other day, because Joel, a Chickasaw friend of mine, said I should, and there in the forty-fourth and forty-fifth paragraphs was "the death's-head hawk moth . . . Acherontia atropos," not exactly Acherontia Styx, the death's head moth of *Silence Of The Lambs* fame, but awfully close.

I was trying to read Didion because someone had told me that I should. I don't remember now exactly what it was I read that Tony Hillerman said about her, but it was very complimentary, in an interview or an essay or something, and so I made a mental note that maybe this is someone I should check into, because I'd been trying to get a handle on Hillerman, and checking into people whose writing he admired seemed one way to go about it.

I've read all of Hillerman's Navajo Tribal Police mysteries, and his volume of essays about New Mexico, and several of his articles in writer's magazines, and his book-length interview with Ernie Bulow, but I have not made up my mind about him yet. I understand Hillerman's books, and Hillerman, himself, is not much of a mystery to me. But I have not made up my mind about him yet.

I don't hold it against Hillerman that he had Jim Chee practicing his sand paintings outside, rather than in a hogan, as according to Ernie Bulow, orthodoxy dictates, just as I don't hold it against Tom Robbins for having his Navajo man painting his pictures in the sand outside of a hogan in the sixth paragraph of *Another Roadside Attraction.*

But I hold it against Didion for this Iago business. Thanks to my trusty *Funk & Wagnalls* I learn that Iago is "the treacherous, scheming villain of Shakespeare's *Othello.*"

I'm immediately consumed by dread. Here's another one of those books that only Joel, or someone like him, could make sense of. He's read all but a handful of Shakespeare's thirty some-odd plays.

My Shakespeare play was *Macbeth.* That was the one that was in our eleventh grade text, and that's the one Mrs. Baugh had us read. I dutifully read every word of it. Had there been another Shakespeare play in the book I would have read it, too, but *Macbeth* was all there was.

At this point I'm beginning to wonder if *Play It As It Lays* is going to be like "The Love Song of J. Alfred Prufrock" or "Wasteland," where you might have had to have read the entire shelf list of Western literature to make sense of it.

Happily, Didion did not end her opening paragraph with that one sentence, and she cannot know the enormity of my gratitude: "What makes Iago evil? some people ask. I never ask."

At this point I am beginning to wonder if she is single and available, so completely have we bonded in spirit, and I read about 110 pages, roughly half of her novel, it going like a whisper on a quiet day, before I remember it was not her fiction that was recommended to me, but her essays.

So I stop reading. I know now that my reading of *Play It As It Lays* will be somewhat leisurely, but this does not necessarily put her novel in bad company. I left Rastignac on the verge of finally about to get laid in *Pere Goriot*, and that was not in this decade either, with every intention of taking Balzac up again. I think about that book now and then, marveling at how anything so poorly written could be so famous. I did fudge and read the last page of it, so I know how it turns out, but frankly I'd rather read about Balzac, himself, who is much more interesting to me than any of his fictional characters I've encountered so far.

Apparently there are others in Oklahoma who have taken a leisurely approach to checking out *Play It As It Lays*. The volume I found in the depths of Bizzell Library at the University of Oklahoma, the only volume, had only been checked out once, due "NOV 26 1985," until my due date of "JUL 29 1992" was stamped.

For a book published in 1970, that's about the pace I suppose the rest of the world would associate with the ebb and flow of intellectual curiosity in these parts (but to be fair, to say nothing of accurate, there was a sticker in the book to the effect it had been purchased from some outfit back East that supplied out-of-print books, so it's possible the particular volume I found had been acquired by OU very near 1985, rather than near 1970).

Hillerman has only been publishing books since about 1970. I didn't discover any of them until the spring of 1991 at a yard sale (got six of them for a dollar), and then I read a total of eleven of his books in the time it takes him to type a chapter. I've not read *Fly On The Wall* yet, or any of his juvenile or picture books. But I intend to, as I've not made up my mind yet about Hillerman.

Didion I'm only beginning to become acquainted with.

Now lest you get the notion I run out and dutifully read everything someone recommends to me, I guess I'll have to admit that I had back-burner forgotten all about Hillerman's recommendation of Didion until I got to reading the introduction to Cornell Woolrich's autobiography, *Blues Of A Lifetime*. The intro was written by the editor, Mark T. Bassett, of the University of Iowa.

Woolrich was one of those *noir* mystery writers who was big in the 40s and the 50s (How big? He left $850,000 to Columbia University in his will). He's been called the fourth man in the hardboiled/*noir* genre, after Dashiell Hammett, Raymond Chandler, and James M. Cain. He's probably most famous in the United States for the movie "Rear Window" which was made from one of his stories. But Woolrich, even though now dead, is a superstar in France because of the ideas in his stories, the view of life that comes through, because of the French literary tradition of Camus, etc. Since the French were, after all, the brothers of the Choctaws for nearly six decades, and the French see things differently than Americans, what Choctaw wouldn't be curious to understand that as much as possible.

Sounds good anyway, huh? Actually I was reading the intro to that book because it was written by the son of a guy I know, an old guy who hangs out at the same coffee shop where I hang out, and this guy, when he was about my age, climbed all the way up the side of Wheeler Peak, the tallest peak in New Mexico, to the very beginnings of the Red River of New Mexico, all the way to Lost Lake, and my Chickasaw friend, Joel, and I had made a whirlwind trip to NE New Mexico just to do that very thing and we didn't even get to Middle Fork Lake up that trail, didn't even get two hundred yards up that trail, from where the automobile road ended at 9,600 feet in elevation, and I was curious to see if there was anything in this old guy's genes that might carry over into literary talent as well as whatever it took to get all the way up that 13,160 ft mountainside.

So there I was reading right along in Bassett's introduction, when all of a sudden, on page xi, he quotes from "Didion's famous essay 'On Keeping A Notebook: My approach to daily life ranges from the grossly negligent to the merely absent-minded . . . .Perhaps it never did snow that August in Vermont; . . . and perhaps no one else felt the ground hardening and summer already dead even as we pretended to bask in it, but that was how it felt to me, and it might have snowed, could have snowed, did snow.'"

Does that not sound like contemporary Native American poetry to you?

I'll tell you, I left the house that instant and drove to Norman and located that December, 1966 issue of *Holiday Magazine*, in which her essay originally appeared, photocopied that essay, took it to the coffee shop and studied it. It was then I began to appreciate what Hillerman must have meant when he had recommended Didion, but then I turned to her fiction, forgetting that it was her essays that had twice now been recommended to me.

I had to put in an inter-library loan request at the Oklahoma County Metropolitan Library System for her volumes of essays because at Oklahoma University they were all on long term loan (several months, which means that faculty have them hoarded).

Sometime soon I'll try to figure out where she published her 1972 essay entitled "The Women's Movement," which, according to the incomplete reference in *Contemporary Authors*, was an essay "dismissing feminism as a 'curious historical anomaly' which has been trivialized by people who did not understand its Marxist roots," and which, again according to *CA*, was answered "In a long and highly critical *Nation* essay, [by] Barbara Grizzuti Harrison." I just love that kind of stuff.

While I patiently await the arrival of those inter-library loan essays, I sometimes think about Hillerman. I think especially about all the disparaging comments I overheard about him at "Returning the Gift: A Festival of North American Native Writers," at the University of Oklahoma,

July 7–10, 1992, an historic gathering of nearly 400 Native literary writers.

Some of the writers I talked to have read Hillerman and like his work. But there were strong voices against him. Curiously, the most vocal, when asked, admitted they had not read him, "nor would I," added one, decisively.

There is a lot of anger in the Native literary world about non-Natives writing about Native cultures, anger at a long succession of anthropologists, Eurocentric historians, Hollywood producers, and now, New Age non-Natives who engage in commercial exploitation of sweat baths and sacred ceremonials.

But I wonder if this anger might be misplaced when aimed at the German-American Hillerman. Perhaps a mixed-blood Choctaw like me might also have no right to say anything about the Navajos. But allow me to cite precedent here. If Geary Hobson, of the University of Oklahoma (a Cherokee-Quapaw-Chickasaw), can praise R.A. Lafferty (an Irish American) for getting the Choctaws right (in Hobson's preface to the OU Press edition of Lafferty's *Okla Hannali*), then I will say, mindful that Hobson was right, and so was Lafferty, that I owe a debt to Hillerman.

I have traveled through Navajo country, lived in the West for a number of years, studied little but 17th century Athapascan history under the late Max L. Moorhead at OU for a couple of years some decades ago, and yet, I believed anthropologist Oliver La Farge, in his 1962 preface to a new issue of his 1929 Pulitzer Prize-winning *Laughing Boy*, when he said that the Navajo culture he had known was a thing of the past.

Hillerman has pointed out, not only to me, but to mainstream America, that Navajos are still with us (news, by the way, which had not reached Oklahoma), and, despite incredible odds, that they are still Navajos. While slouching around here in town, waiting for one thing and another, not the least of which is Hillerman's next book, having not made up my mind yet about Hillerman, that strikes me as counting for something.

Lonesome Duck
The Blueing Of A
Texas-American Myth

▼ ▼ ▼ ▼ ▼ ▼ ▼ ▼ ▼ ▼ ▼ ▼ ▼ ▼ ▼

There is a line of dialogue in *Hud* in which Homer Bannon (played by Melvyn Douglas in an Academy Award-winning role), standing like a patriarch of grandfatherly wisdom at the foot of a staircase in a ranch house on the West Texas plains, delivers a bit of Hollywood screenplay cornpone philosophy to his grandson: "Little by little," says old Homer, "the look of the country changes because of the men we admire."

Hollywood cornpone or not, one can learn something about a people by examining the men they admire. One can learn something about Texans and Texas by this method.

In May, 1965, When President Lyndon Johnson was asked to write a foreword to a University of Texas Press edition of Houghton Mifflin's 1935 monumental 584-page work of history, *The Texas Rangers: A Century Of Frontier Defense*, by Walter Prescott Webb, an edition printed from the original plates, identical in every regard except for some minor changes in the frontmatter, among them the substitution of Lyndon Johnson's foreword for a couple of pieces of poetry, The Texas Ranger singled out for special mention by the President of the United States, himself a Texan, was Captain L.H. McNelly.

The President writes: "Captain McNelly was one of the

most effective of the Texas Rangers . . . [He] repeatedly told his men that 'courage is a man who keeps on coming on.' As Dr. Webb would explain to me, 'you can slow a man like that, but you can't defeat him—the man who keeps on coming on is either going to get there himself or make it possible for a later man to reach the goal'" (x).

Captain McNelly does indeed keep on coming on. His exploits have a special appeal to Texans, even to scholars steeped in Greek philosophy and German poetry, such as Craig Clifford. As an unemployed PhD living in Maryland, having spent many years away from Texas, Clifford was so amazed at the power of McNelly, speaking to contemporary Texans across a century of time, that Clifford was moved to wonder if he could learn something about himself, moved to ask: could he "learn who he is by reading how Captain L.H. McNelly crossed the Rio Grande with thirty Texas Rangers in 1875 against all orders of the U.S. authorities?" Clifford discovered "when I read how McNelly told a U.S. Cavalry officer that he didn't object to his men sitting down with him because he wouldn't fight alongside anyone he didn't believe his equal, I knew a little better than I did before why I'm the way I am" (Clifford 13–14).

What was it, one might ask, that Captain McNelly did in 1875 that so stirs the hearts of Texans a century later, whether they be a President of the United States or an unemployed PhD.? Perhaps the following quotation can shed light on that question:

> . . . Early in 1875 McNelly and his men were sent into the infamous Nueces Strip, that portion of Texas lying between the Nueces River and the Rio Grande. McNelly's job was to rid the area of cattle thieves, of which there were a great many. He did a brilliant, brave job, and his methods were absolutely ruthless. Any Mexican unlucky enough to be caught was tortured until he coughed up information, then summarily hung. Mexicans found with cattle were shot. In one of his boldest moves, McNelly

and his thirty men crossed the Rio Grande to attack a ranch near Las Cuevas, where some 250 Mexican soldiers were assembled. Unfortunately the Rangers dashed into the wrong ranch and found a number of men working at the woodpile, cutting wood while their wives cooked breakfast. The Rangers shot them down, then realized their mistake and went on to the right ranch. Whether apologies were offered to the wives of the slain woodchoppers is not recorded. Webb is aware that McNelly's methods might conceivably be criticized, but he satisfies himself with the remark that 'Affairs on the border cannot be judged by standards that hold elsewhere.'

Why they can't is a question apologists for the Rangers have yet to answer. Torture is torture, whether inflicted in Germany, Algiers, or along the Nueces Strip. The Rangers, of course, claimed that their end justified their means, but people who practice torture always claim that. Since the practical end, in this case, was the recovery of a few hundred cattle, one might dispute the claim. Only a generation or two earlier the Nueces Strip had been Mexico, and it is not inconceivable that some of the Mexicans involved had as good a right to the cattle as Captain Richard King or any other Texas cattleman (McMurtry, "Southwestern Literature?" *In A Narrow Grave: Essays On Texas* 40–41).

As is evident from the content of the above passage, its author, Larry McMurtry, is a perceptive and provocative critic of Texas letters. In the above essay he practically invents literary controversy in Texas. He does the unthinkable. He desecrates the hallowed names of J. Frank Dobie, Roy Bedichek, and Walter Prescott Webb, taking them one at a time and seriously damaging their reputations as men of letters. Texas letters has never been the same. (For some idea of the stature of these men and the courage required to do what McMurtry did, see the memorial testimonials in *Three Men In Texas: Bedichek, Webb, and Dobie; Essays By Their Friends In The Texas Observer*, edited by Ronnie Dugger, U of Texas P, 1967).

McMurtry's stature as a critic of Texas letters is the equal of his reputation as a novelist, at least within Texas. As Ernestine P. Sewell reports, for his attack on Dobie, Bedichek, and Webb, "McMurtry was labeled the enfant terrible of Texas letters" (Reynolds 318). Jose E. Limon calls McMurtry "the foremost of the few critics of 'Texas literature'" (Clifford and Pilkington 59).

McMurtry's willingness to find fault with the work of fellow Texas writers was first manifested in 1968 in his essay "Southwestern Literature?" Lest Texans forget the main themes of that essay, he followed it up with a scathing lecture (in which he refers to Dobie, Bedichek, and Webb as "the Holy Oldtimers"), delivered in person at the Fort Worth Art Museum in September, 1981, entitled "Ever a Bridegroom: Reflections On The Failure Of Texas Literature," which was published in the October 23, 1981 issue of the *Texas Observer* and reprinted in 1989 by SMU Press in *Range Wars: Heated Debates, Sober Reflections, and Other Assessments of Texas Writing*, edited by Craig Clifford and Tom Pilkington, in which McMurtry adds a 1987 postscript to his essay.

McMurtry's essays, and his novels, and the movies made from those novels, led to a rather thick tome, also published by SMU Press in 1989, entitled *Taking Stock: A Larry McMurtry Casebook*, edited by Clay Reynolds, in which practically all of Texas takes turns telling what they consider to be wrong with Larry McMurtry.

Nowhere among any of this literature does one find a Native American viewpoint (though Louise Erdrich does offer a review of *Texasville*, a novel and movie not concerned with Indians). Not only does McMurtry fail to voice any concern with the way Indians are dealt with in Texas literature, but the considerable body of rebuttal to McMurtry's criticisms is also silent on the topic.

When McMurtry wrote "Southwestern Literature?" in 1968 he was a young English instructor who had been teaching at Texas Christian University and at Rice Institute. He had gained a reputation as Texas' most promising novelist with the publication of his first three novels: *Horseman, Pass By* (1961; filmed as *Hud* in 1963); *Leaving Cheyenne* (1963; filmed as *Lovin' Molly* in 1974); and *The Last Picture Show* (1966; filmed under the same name in 1971).

In preparation for writing "Southwestern Literature?" McMurtry read the entire canon of Dobie, Bedichek, and Webb, twenty-nine books in all, twenty-two of them by Dobie. All three men were recently deceased. They comprised The Big Three of Texas letters, Dobie the anecdotal worshipper of things rural, Bedichek the naturalist, and Webb the historian of the West.

McMurtry finds Dobie and Bedichek irrelevant to the experience of modern, urban Texas. "For my generation," he writes " . . . I doubt we could scrape up enough nature-lore between us to organize a decent picnic" (36). That is among his more gentle observations, as he then sets about dissecting the work of the two nature lovers, being harshest on Dobie.

After warming up on Bedichek, and before getting to Dobie, McMurtry takes up the case of Walter Prescott Webb, the late, revered professor of history at the University of Texas. McMurtry's critical acumen is not nearly so penetrating when applied to the history of the West, which he makes evident by his fairly reverent attitude toward Webb's books on the subject, particularly *The Great Frontier*.

Webb was an uncritical disciple of Frederick Jackson Turner's "Frontier Hypothesis," in which the westward movement of Anglo-Americans, particularly their complete inability to be restrained and their disregard for the rights of indigenous peoples, somehow becomes a thing filled with great promise for the earth.

But McMurtry can spot a "glaring whitewash" (40) when he reads one, and thus he focuses his attack on Webb's *The Texas Rangers*.

McMurtry is appalled at the racism and violence of the Rangers, but even more so at Webb's blindness to it. McMurtry writes: "His own facts about the Rangers contradict again and again his characterization of them as 'quiet, deliberate, gentle' men" (40). McMurtry cites a number of examples similar to the quotation above concerning Captain McNelly in 1875, all regarding the Rangers' relations with Hispanics or Blacks, including Captain Bill McDonald's speech as he advanced on men accused of being the Ft. Brown rioters in 1906: "'You niggers hold up there! I'm Captain McDonald . . . and I'm down here to investigate a foul murder you scoundrels have committed. I'll show you niggers something you've never been used to . . . '" (42).

McMurtry indicts Webb for failing to censure the Rangers' "racial arrogance," for his willingness "to accept the still common assumption that a Ranger can tell whether a Mexican is honest or dishonest simply by looking at him," and laments that "the same method was used to separate good Negroes from bad" (42). Throughout McMurtry's attack it is telling that he has nothing to say about the Texas Rangers' attitude regarding Indians or the glee with which Walter Prescott Webb reports the genocidal activities of the Texas Rangers against Indians.

McMurtry is not alone among critics of Texas letters in not having it occur to them to mention Indians when discussing the failures of Texas literature. Celia Morris, in a keynote address delivered at a Texas women scholars' conference held at the University of Texas at Austin in the spring of 1986, while finding fault with the way men portray women in Texas literature, says, "I find little hint, really, of the Texas women—black, brown, or white—whom I know best in any of this writing . . . And If I, a white woman close to some of those male writers, find their work alien, I have no trouble imagining how remote it must seem to black women and Chicanas" (Clifford and Pilkington 107–108).

Indians, women and men alike, find it very remote indeed. Texas writers seem to be incapable of thinking of Indians as Texans. The image is too jarring to the soul to be admitted. To Texans, Indians have always been a part of Nature; they are sub-human. They are also past tense. They were a "barrier" (Rupert Norval Richardson's term), or they committed "depredations" (J.W. Wilbarger's term). They were dealt with long ago, and, like the buffalo herds, they are gone now; no need to dwell on why or how that happened, unless, of course, Hollywood might be interested.

In that case the moviegoer will be treated to scenes of heroic "settlers" fighting off attacks by redskinned horseback sub-humans. Somehow the Indians manage to get portrayed as the invaders and the "settlers" get portrayed as the ones defending the invasion of their homeland. If the action takes place in Texas it will likely take place in West Texas, as though somehow that was the only part of Texas that had any Indians, and the Indians will not have any more sense than to ride around in circles until a sufficient number of them have been shot. One is left to assume that the Indians continued to ride around in circles until they all got shot, and that is how Texas ended up without any redskinned sub-humans. (For an entertaining survey of how Indians have been portrayed by Hollywood, see *Shadows Of The Indian* by Raymond William Stedman, U of Oklahoma P, 1982).

The truth of the matter in Texas is far more interesting than fiction but is something Hollywood has not yet gotten around to exploring.

Edward S. Curtis, in volume 19 of *The North American Indian*, succinctly states the Texas attitude regarding Indians: "Texas was generous in respect to its aboriginal inhabitants, being ever willing to give its Indians to any one who might want them. In fact, the Texas mandate, though not recorded in the statutes was, 'Go elsewhere or be exterminated'" (36).

The student desiring a brief summary of how Texas managed to rid itself of its aboriginal inhabitants well before the end of the nineteenth century, with the exception of the ninety-seven acre Isleta del Sur Pueblo near El Paso and the Alabama-Coushatta in East Texas, is referred to Chapter 13, "Extermination and Oblivion," in *The Indians of Texas: From Prehistoric to Modern Times*, by W.W. Newcomb, Jr. (U of Texas P, 1961). One might note particularly that it made no difference whatsoever whether the Native peoples were hostile or friendly, nomadic or sedentary, whether they lived on the high plains, the central plains, the eastern woodlands, or along the Gulf shore, whether they attempted to reside peacefully on land specifically set aside for them, or whether they were allies of Texas, even if they had supplied fighting men to help champion the Texas cause against other Indians. They were not wanted; they were not tolerated; they were driven out of Texas or they were exterminated.

At least one prominent official who attempted to intervene on behalf of the Indians was murdered—Texas Superintendent of Indian Affairs, Robert S. Neighbors, who committed the offense of hurriedly ushering his charges out of state in 1859 to save them from being exterminated by angry mobs who did not care to attempt any distinction between peaceful and hostile Indians. These Indians numbered about 1,500, with 1,000 of them being mostly Caddo, Anadarko, Ioni, Waco, and Tonkawa from the Brazos reservation, and about 500 of them being Penateka Comanches from a smaller reservation nearby. They were forced to abandon nearly all their possessions and livestock on more than 70,000 acres, where they had pursued an agricultural and range cattle economy, and where they had, in fact, been allies of Texas in armed engagements against other Indians. Neighbors made the mistake of returning to Texas where he met with vigilante justice, a shotgun blast in the back (Richardson, *Texas* 152; Utley 135–138; Wallace and Hoebel 302).

The Cherokees, Delawares, Kickapoos, Seminoles, Shawnees, and other Native peoples from east of the Mississippi, who had migrated to the headwaters of the Sabine, where they established agricultural communities, made the mistake of residing on rich land coveted by the East Texans. In 1838 they were summarily ordered to leave. When they refused, they were driven from Texas in two bloody engagements, finding themselves relentlessly pursued until they had crossed the Red River into the Choctaw and Chickasaw Nations (Newcomb 347).

The Karankawas of the Gulf Coast, hemmed in on all sides, unable to flee and unwilling to attempt much of an accommodation with the Texans, were exterminated (Newcomb 341–343). One can seek out the fate of any particular Native people in Texas, but with the exception of the Alabama-Coushatta, the story has the same ending; they were exterminated or they were driven out.

Not until the twentieth century did Indians begin returning to Texas, where they remain practically invisible, clustered in the state's urban centers, where they struggle with the problems of urban Indians everywhere, stripped of their land base, isolated from their scattered people, aliens in their native land (Arkeketa, "Returning The Gift" panel discussion). Being invisible, they are ignored. When they are not invisible they are not appreciated.

On the weekend of March 13–15, 1992, the Texas chapter of the American Indian Movement organized a Columbus protest march in Corpus Christi, Texas. The *Micmac News*, a Canadian Indian publication, had correspondents on the scene, who report: "One noteworthy incident occurred which caused a lot of bad feelings. A Corpus Christi police captain, in speaking to a member of the press, stated: 'The FBI thinks of AIM as Assholes In Moccassins,' and make it clear that he shared that same opinion. AIM demanded a full apology, which was not given immediately. The captain was given a 10-day suspension—with pay—from the police department (punishment or reward?). This type of racist comment is inexcusable from a person in his position and might have had an influence on the gun threats the demonstrators received. Eventually an apology was published in the local press" (Cape and Dedam 20).

"'We were closely watched by the FBI, the Texas Rangers, and the National Guard,'" said Santos Suarez, head of the Texas chapter of AIM, "' . . . but we were not there to try anything foolish, just there to inform the people of the truth about Columbus. We had no sound system so we had to shout our speeches to get our message across. On the second day, they tried to drown us out with a rock concert'" (Cape and Dedam 20).

Not all Texans were Indian haters bent on driving all Indians out of Texas. The Indians had a friend in Sam Houston. During his terms of office as president of the republic of Texas and as governor of the state of Texas he attempted to accommodate the needs of Indians in Texas governmental policy. As previously noted, Robert S. Neighbors lost his life in saving the lives of the people of the Brazos reservation. Other prominent Texans, such as frontier physician and naturalist Dr. Gideon Lincecum, were deeply interested in Indian culture. Before moving to Texas shortly after Texas became a state, Lincecum had been a student of Choctaw language and culture in Mississippi. Late in life he contributed a valuable biography of Choctaw Chief Pushmataha, as well as other observations about Chcotaw culture in transition which are available nowhere else (Lincecum's contributions were published early in the twentieth century in the *Publications Of The Mississippi Historical Society*). It might also be noted that one of the most sympathetic and knowledgeable students of Choctaw culture, H. B. Cushman, who grew up among the Choctaws of Mississippi early in the nineteenth century as the son of American Board missionaries to the Choctaws, spent his mature years as a resident of Texas (Cushman's *History of the Choctaw, Chickasaw, and Nathez Indians*, 1899, is a cherished document for students of Choctaw history).

But men such as these were a distinct minority in Texas. Even Sam Houston, while president of the Republic of Texas, was unable to persuade the Texas senate to ratify the treaty he had negotiated on February 25, 1836, with the Sabine River communities of Eastern Indians. In 1838 Houston's successor, Mirabeau Lamar, moved quickly to drive those communities out of Texas (Newcomb 347; Everett 100–109).

When another man such as Mirabeau Lamar, Hardin R. Runnels, became governor of the state of Texas on December 21, 1857, matters took a grim turn for the Indians. Official Texas policy became one of genocidal attack upon Indians, even if the Indians were to be found living outside the boundaries of Texas. The Texas legislature approved the creation of a new company of one hundred Texas Rangers specifically designated for offensive operations (Webb, *The Texas Rangers* 151; Huges 130–131).

Genocidal attacks upon Indian villages have now become well known events. In recent decades the conduct of Colonel John M. Chivington and his Colorado Volunteers at the Sand Creek Massacre in 1864 and of Lieutenant Colonel George Armstrong Custer's Seventh U.S. Cavalry at the "Battle" of the Washita in 1868 have become cliches in the history of the West. Much less well known within American popular culture is the role of Texas and the Texas Rangers in demonstrating that Plains Indians were vulnerable to such attacks.

United States Army policy in Texas had been one of maintaining a defensive line of fortifications stretching across West Texas (see Utley, *Frontiersmen In Blue: The United States Army And The Indian, 1848–1865*, U of Nebraska P, 1981). This policy changed quickly after the Texas Rangers demonstrated that Plains Indian villages filled with women and children were in no way defensible military fortifications.

Governor Runnels found his man in Ranger Captain John S. (Rip) Ford. Runnels appointed him Senior Captain in charge of all Texas forces and commissioned him to pursue the Indians to wherever he might find them, brooking no interference from the United States or anyone else. With 102 Texas Rangers, most of them armed with two Colt pistols and a muzzle-loading rifle, giving them an estimated firepower of fifteen hundred rounds without reloading, and with an equal or slightly greater number of Indian auxiliaries from the Brazos reservation under the command of Captain Shapley P. Ross, Ford crossed the Red River into present-day Oklahoma, and, in the early morning hours of May 12, 1858, attacked without warning and destroyed a Comanche village on the north bank of the Canadian River near the Antelope Hills, killing seventy-six people (Webb, *The Texas Rangers* 151–158; Hughes 129–149).

Regarding this attack, Rupert Norval Richardson writes, in *The Comanche Barrier To South Plains Settlement: A Century And A Half Of Savage Resistance To The Advancing White Frontier*:

> The village which was destroyed was that of a band of Kotsoteka or Buffalo-eater Comanches. The fact that there were no "American" horses among the three hundred or more head which Ford and Ross took from the village indicates that this Comanche band had not recently committed depredations on the Texas settlements. Ford does not state the number of women and children among the seventy-six Indians slain, for that was a matter of no great concern to the Texas people . . .
>
> A singular characteristic of the Ford-Ross campaign is that it was carried out by Texas forces, acting on state authority only, yet operating and fighting a battle outside of the state. In this regard, the officers take no notice of the fact that the battle with the Indians was not fought on Texas soil, and the boundary line evidently was a matter of little concern to them. The Indians had been defeated; the place of the engagement and the means used were items of little consequence. As one enthusiastic citizen wrote the president: 'The rangers, with the assistance of the friendly Indians, killed seventy wild Indians. When did the soldiers ever do as much?' (236–237).

Contemplating this genocide, Walter Prescott Webb writes:

> In Ford's eyes the campaign was of much importance. It had demonstrated that the Indians could be followed, found, and defeated in their own country; it proved that the buffalo ranges beyond Red River could be penetrated and held by white men. Ford might have

added—and he may have had in mind—that what was most needed for such undertakings was a leader with brains and courage. Texas had not lacked men to follow; what it had lacked for ten years or more was a Texas Ranger with brains supported by a governor with enough internal fortitude to back him up. Ford and his men had rescued an ideal (*The Texas Rangers* 158).

There is something strikingly similar about Ranger Captain Ford dashing into an Indian village outside of Texas in 1858, killing people with whom Texas may have had no quarrel, and Ranger Captain McNelly dashing into a Mexican ranch outside of Texas in 1875, killing people with whom Texas may have had no quarrel.

There is also an important difference. While Captain McNelly's attack did not inspire others to follow his example, Captain Ford's attack showed the United States Army how to deal with Plains Indians. It was a lesson the Army was not long in taking to heart.

Major General David E. Twiggs, of the U.S. Army's Department of Texas, was inspired by the example set before him. "'For the last ten years we have been on the defensive,' he wrote to General [Winfield] Scott on July 6. Now it was time to abandon this policy, invade the Indian homeland, 'and follow them up winter and summer, thus giving the Indians something to do at home in taking care of their families, and they might possibly let Texas alone'" (Utley 130).

On October 1 of that same year, 1858, acting on orders from General Twiggs, Major Earl Van Dorn, leading a force of United States Cavalry out of Texas into present-day Oklahoma, attacked and destroyed a joint encampment of Wichitas and Comanches near the present town of Rush Springs (Utley 130–132).

Unknown to General Twiggs and Major Van Dorn, these Indians had just concluded an agreement of peace and friendship with officers from Fort Arbuckle of the U.S. Army's Department of the West. General Twiggs and Mayor

Van Dorn were embarrassed by this difficulty in following the Texas Rangers' example of shooting first and asking questions later. Their response was to urge that the Army put a stop to such treaty making . Early the next year Major Van Dorn carried out another attack from Texas, this time on Comanches in present-day southern Kansas (Utley 132–135).

The beginning of the end for the Plains Indians, at least on the Southern Plains, can be traced to this genocidal military tactic of the Texas Rangers, first demonstrated in the spring of 1858. Many other factors would be important in the destruction of the Plains Indians' way of life, among them the eventual slaughter of the buffalo herds upon which their culture depended. But the vulnerability of their women and children in their villages played a significant role in breaking their will to resist (Wallace and Hoebel 302).

No one today would think of attempting to portray Colonel Chivington as a hero in a work of literature. Chivington's massacre at Sand Creek is regarded as one of those "unfortunate" events in the American past.

Likewise, the reputation of Colonel Custer has not fared well in modern times for the same reasons. The unflattering portrait of Custer in the film *Little Big Man*, in which "Custer is portrayed as the psychotic he clearly was" (Scheuer 416), is likely to be the best he can hope for.

How can it be, then, that the foremost critic of Texas letters, a person who is quite likely the state's most talented novelist, can write a novel glorifying two mid-nineteenth century ex-Rangers? These "heroes" are men who, so their fictional resume states, were high-ranking leaders of the Texas Rangers at the time of that seminally important genocidal attack in 1858, and who, by age and circumstance, would have been a part of that attack or would have engaged in similar conduct.

How can it be that such a choice of heroes can be so taken to the heart of the American public that the book should receive the Pulitzer Prize in literature and become a tremendously successful television mini-series?

Are such men worthy candidates for canonization as American heroes? How can an author such as Larry Mc-Murtry, who is sensitive to racially prejudicial material in Texas literature regarding Blacks and Hispanics, be callous where the sensitivities of Native American people are concerned? Yet, it is Larry McMurtry who has given us *Lonesome Dove*.

As a 1985 novel it received not only the Pulitzer Prize but a Spur Award by the Western Writers of America as well as the Texas Institute of Letters Prize for fiction. In 1989 it held the viewing public spellbound as a television mini-series, and since then it has reached millions of viewers on video cassette, both by purchase and rental of the cassettes.

In *Lonesome Dove* McMurtry has given us Captain Augustus McCrae and Captain Woodrow F. Call, aging, former Texas Rangers, veterans of twenty-one "engagements" with the Comanches and Kiowas, civilians now for about ten years, struggling to find a place in the world, in an Indian-less Texas, in the aftermath of their Ranger service. They will get up a herd of cattle and horses, which they steal from Mexican ranches in a sort of tongue in cheek tit for tat, and drive them to Montana.

They are a lovable pair, indeed. They poke fun at one another's habits, argue about the propriety of keeping a pair of pet pigs, and generally bask in the glory of their Ranger days. In their relations with Indians they conduct themselves in a politically correct manner by contemporary standards, thereby endearing themselves to modern audiences and perpetuating myth. They give cattle to starving Northern Indians who they encounter on the cattle drive, pathetically suggesting that the Indians would have met a kinder, gentler fate if only there had been a few more Texas Rangers on the scene a decade or two earlier.

Why not pick Paraguay for a setting and put Joseph Mengele in the cattle business; he could cut out a few head of cattle and give them to a Jewish orphan's home, thereby endearing himself to readers and TV mini-series viewers in Tel Aviv and New York and Dallas. Better yet, why not write speculative fiction. Imagine a scenario in which Hitler manages an armistice that allows his regime to remain in power. His aging Nazi Storm Troopers could become figures of romantic heroism in contemporary literature. If a novelist of sufficient talent were to take up the task, infusing his characters with an engaging comraderie, there might be a Pulitzer Prize in it.

One is reminded that it is McMurtry in his essay "Southwestern Literature?" who finds nothing worthy of comment about the manner in which the Texas Rangers operated against Indians or the manner in which Walter Prescott Webb reports the genocidal conduct of the Texas Rangers toward Indians. Reading Webb with a critical eye, McMurtry passes over in silence Webb's description of this conduct as having "rescued an ideal," of requiring "brains" and "internal fortitude," and his conclusion that Texas had wasted "ten years or more" waiting for the right combination of Ranger and governor to make such activity possible.

Among the things overlooked by McMurtry in *The Texas Rangers* is Webb's report of "the last real Indian fight on Texas soil" (403) in January, 1881. Webb's idea of a "real Indian fight" is for a detachment of sixteen Texas Rangers under the command of Ranger Captain George W. Baylor, augmented by an unspecified number of Rangers under the command of Ranger Lieutenant C.L. Nevill, to sneak up on an Apache encampment of twelve men, four women, and four children, and, at dawn, shoot the women and children. Webb explains: "The warriors were the first to run off, and the result was that the women and children were the chief sufferers. Baylor explained that it was a bitterly cold, windy morning, and as the Indians all wore blankets, it was impossible to tell women from men. 'In fact,' he added, 'the law under which the Frontier Battalion was organized don't require it'" (405).

Members of this Apache band may have killed a small

detachment of soldiers, some isolated herders, and some travelers. Materials found at their camp—one might add, found after the shooting—principally some cavalry equipment, including saddles and a pistol, satisfied the Rangers, and Webb, and apparently McMurtry, that they had found the group of Indians they sought. It apparently did not occur to them that this group of Indians may have traded for the materials or otherwise come into their possession innocently. The Apaches were not given an opportunity to respond to any charges, even though the Rangers under Captain Baylor had admittedly lost the trail of the group they had been attempting to follow for several days, a trail that wound in and out of Mexico, from the scene of an attack on a stagecoach. They had, in fact, given up on trying to follow the trail and had fallen in with Lieutenant Nevill and his men who had found a trail on the other side of the mountains, which may or may not have been the same group of Indians (403-406). In any event it is not clear what crime the children were thought to have committed.

One is reminded of McMurtry's reverence for Webb's *The Great Frontier*, which, despite its title, is actually an examination of the impact upon the Old World of having brought the New World within its orb. To facilitate the discussion he wants to present, without being pestered by matters he considers irrelevant, Webb explains that Indians are not people, not really, not real people the way Americans are people; Indians are "primitive" (3); and they are not really there, anyway; the land is "empty" (3); "the American experience" was one of "sole proprietor of an unsettled contiguous territory" (3); and since Indians are not really there, the best thing for them is to brush them aside into a footnote.

Despite whatever sort of blindness it may have been that afflicted Walter Prescott Webb as an historian, and despite whatever shortcomings Larry McMurtry may have as a critic, McMurtry's talents as a novelist are something to reckon with.

Texas Rangers who were in active service in the middle

of the nineteenth century do not deserve to be portrayed as anything other than villains in works of literature. It is open to question whether Texas Rangers of any era deserve much in the way of sympathetic treatment. (For a recent reappraisal of the Texas Rangers, see Samora, et al, *Gunpowder Justice*, U of Notre Dame P, 1979, which does not take into account Ford's genocidal Ranger attack in 1858).

Hollywood does not seem capable of portraying the Texas Rangers in any way other than the hero worship evident in such films as *The Comancheros*, with John Wayne. But there are novelists who have had no difficulty discerning the character of these men and conveying it to their readers. John Prebble is one such novelist.

In *The Buffalo Soldiers*, a novel concerned primarily with the relationships between a White cavalry officer, his Black Civil War-veteran troopers, and a small group of reservation Comanches which the soldiers are escorting on a buffalo hunt on the plains just north of Texas, Prebble renders a memorable portrait of a troop of thirty-five Texas Rangers when they put in an appearance at the Red River. The Rangers kill one of the Comanches when he ventures across the river to hunt deer (49–53; Prebble apparently bases this incident on the death of Au-to-tainte, a Kiowa who was killed by the Texas Rangers under the same circumstances, see Nye 354).

Prebble gives a close-up view of two Ranger officers when they cross the river to try to intimidate the Army into standing aside. Angered that the cavalry officer and his troopers will not allow the force of Rangers to cross the river to kill the rest of the Comanche buffalo hunters, the Rangers hurl insults, "nigger" being prominent among them, and alternately try to goad the troopers or the Comanches into giving the Rangers an excuse for crossing the river in force (49–53).

In addition to novelists such as John Prebble, scholars such as Ernestine P. Sewell have no difficulty assessing the character of the Texas Rangers. She says of them flatly,

" . . . they were violent, ruthless men who thought all non-whites to be sub-human" (Reynolds 318).

McMurtry might have done a service to the reading public, and by extension to the television-viewing public, if he had obtained a vision of these men as profound as the one which John Prebble achieved.

Lonesome Dove would be a different book and the television mini-series would be a different viewing experience, but it might not have been necessary to change the story, except for the motivations, inner thoughts, and interpretations of the characters.

It might not be too late even now to see what sort of story McMurtry might have told. Since it is acceptable to distort history, why not distort it grossly by giving his two main characters a conscience, a real conscience, something other than an ethnocentristic conscience. After all, if Addo-eette, known as Big Tree, who as a young Kiowa had participated prominently in the Salt Creek Massacre of 1871, could say late in life that he deeply regretted the things he had done in his youth (Nye 317), perhaps it is not so far-fetched to imagine that two old ex-Rangers might find discomfort in memories from their past.

Other than this change, it might be possible to remain faithful to McMurtry's storyline and situations in all other respects. Such a story might be titled *Lonesome Duck.*

In *Lonesome Duck* one would find the same emptiness on the plains of West Texas that is central to McMurtry's story. The Southern buffalo herds are gone, slaughterd by commercial hunters, leaving behind only millions and millions of bones.

Gone too are the Indians. The Texas Rangers and the U.S. Army have done their jobs, having swept down on villages filled with women and children until even the most courageous freedom fighters became convinced that the savage invaders would exterminate them if they continued to defend their homeland.

In this momentary vacuum, before greedy, land grabbing cattle ranchers have completed the dispossession of the landscape, the sweeping away of organized Indian life has left the stage to a new form of being—the renegade—young men estranged from their people, from their culture, from their way of life. Their time will be short upon the earth. They will not perpetuate themselves, will not propagate and see themselves recreated in their children. They will be outlaws for a time, a unique creation of Texas and American Indian policy, and then they will die violent deaths and be gone. Their companions will be another endangered species on the brink of extinction, shiftless Comancheros, now out of business since there are no longer any Indians with whom to conduct illicit trade.

Dominating this empty landscape is a half-breed, renegade outlaw named Blue Duck, an aberration, a monster created by the Texas Rangers as much as by anyone else, a sociopath who occupies himself raiding the ranches of the invading Texans, looting, burning, murdering, raping, plundering, stealing children at will, and retreating to the vastness of the Llano Estacado. When Blue Duck leaves his isolated, lonely camps, he leaves behind no vulnerable loved ones. The Texas Rangers do not know how to deal with him. He can travel farther and faster without water on the arid landscape than they can. He is everywhere and nowhere. The Rangers are frustrated nearly to tears at their inability to do anything about him.

Unable to stop Blue Duck—not just unable to catch him, but unable even to get a good look at him—one group of Rangers has quit. Feeling the sting of the way the Texas myth hates a quitter (a myth so strong it would still be alive a century later, demanding its brutal sacrifices at the alter of the football practice field at the University of Texas, ably described by Gary Shaw in *Meat On The Hoof*), these "retired" Rangers have huddled together on the banks of the lower Rio Grande, in the lower Rio Grande Valley, about as far from the rest of Texas as one can get.

They were famous once, but now they'd just as soon not explain why they're not Rangering anymore or what they do with themselves these days.

Captain Augustus McCrae has become an alcoholic. A decade of whiskey-soaked afternoons and evenings has left him able to do little but hold a deck of cards into the wee hours of the morning and then make biscuits.

Ten years of sloshing in whiskey makes a man's hands tremble.

Captain Woodrow F. Call seeks solace in non-stop work. The burr under his saddle is a big one. He cannot forget the times when he was judge, jury, and executioner, all on a single day. Faces of dead Indian children torment him. He fears that some power greater than Texas will call upon him to answer for his actions. Void of any sense of humor, cold and distant to all who know him, dangerous to anyone who doesn't, he sits in solitude each evening cleaning his rifle and guarding the river, just in case.

Reduced to stealing for a living, they have become horse and cattle, and probably, pig thieves, raiding other ranches within the watershed of the Rio Grande without energy, ambition, or purpose.

Pea Eye, like the faithful ex-Ranger corporal he is, is devoted to his captain, Woodrow F. Call, and is too slow a thinker to realize the man is haunted by his past.

An unlikely Black ex-Ranger scout, Joshua Deets, is just there, having nowhere else to go. He waits for the day when Captain Call will again need a scout and ruminates by moonlight on the mysteries of a White Man's Texas.

Newt, the orphaned son of a long-dead whore and take-your-pick one of the men of the household, has grown to early manhood here, idolizing, and being over-protected by, Woodrow F. perhaps-his-father Call, learning black-smithing from the corporal, being buddies with the Black scout, and receiving his education by listening to the whiskey words of Augustus McCrae, who fancies himself a philosopher.

An aged, diabetic, retired, Mexican-bandit cook named Boliver rounds out the household, which is situated across a dry wash from Lonesome Dove, which has a small dusty barroom with one whore, a store, another building or two, and little else.

Into this graveyard of Texas honor rides a long-lost former member of the Ranger troop, Jake Spoon, now a gambler on the run from what passes for the law in Fort Smith, Arkansas, not the federal boys, Judge Parker's *True Grit*/John Wayne/Rooster Cogburns, but the indecisive, tenderly emotional sheriff of Fort Smith, July Johnson, and his dimwit deputy, Roscoe Brown.

Spoon has seen the grasslands of Montana, where the Indians are still burdened by the vulnerability of defenseless loved ones, and now that the U.S. Army has gotten around to them, having recently buried Colonel George Armstrong Custer, these men know what will happen next. Woodrow F. Call determines to move into the vacuum, "before the bankers and lawyers get it," and become the first man to graze cattle in Montana. He will get up a herd, stolen from other ranchers, and drive them there.

Augustus McCrae, alcoholic, whoremongering horse and cattle thief, and idle-about, penny ante gambler, carrying around a memory of himself now laughably at odds with the truth, decides to go along as far as Ogallala, Nebraska, to make one last effort to woo and win a woman perceptive enough to have seen him for what he was and what he would become, fifteen years earlier.

McCrae and Call forget that between where they stand and where they hope to go lies the range of Blue Duck.

On the trail, having had this grand stage properly prepared for him, Blue Duck takes time off from his work of ridding the landscape of one land grabbing Texan after another, and rides boldly into camp, not the cattle drive camp, but the satellite camp of the Lonesome Dove whore, who is tagging along, nominally with Jake Spoon, trying to make her way to San Francisco.

Augustus McCrae is visiting the whore, and he barely has time to strap on a six-gun as his worst nightmare comes riding up.

Blue Duck faces down McCrae and takes what he

wants, a drink of water from the river. He has nothing but contempt for a "worn out old Ranger."

With the honor of Texas hanging in the balance, McCrae does what he does best, nothing. The moment passes, and the opportunity is gone when Blue Duck rides away.

Energized by the frantic denial of the deep look he has had into his soul, McCrae performs superhuman feats when Blue Duck returns and steals the Lonesome Dove whore. McCrae almost convinces himself that the yellow in his laundry can be counteracted by just a touch of blueing agent. If only he can catch and kill Blue Duck, honor will be restored.

A lot of killing does take place, including a few shiftless Comancheros and the renegade Kiowas in Blue Duck's gang. McCrae retrieves the Lonesome Dove whore, but she's been abused beyond the immediate recovery of her senses.

Blue Duck leaves McCrae with one more reminder that he should have stayed on his shady porch in South Texas. While McCrae and Sheriff July Johnson, who has teamed up with McCrae, are a few miles away killing Blue Duck's drunken, renegade Kiowas, Blue Duck is butchering the ones they left behind, Johnson's nitwit deputy and a boy and a girl, reminding McCrae, with all the irony of a sick sort of poetic justice, of how the Texans "whipped" the Indians.

Haunted by the memory of his encounter with Blue Duck, and all the old Ranger memories that encounter rekindled, McCrae continues on to Nebraska, only to learn that the woman of his dreams is not in the market for a retired mass murderer. In Montana, having come to the end of his string, McCrae chooses suicide when an infection from arrow wounds offers him a choice between death from blood poisoning or having both of his legs cut off, which would reduce him physically to his actual stature in the West.

He chooses to be remembered by the myth of his younger days, when others, especially Texans, honored killers of women and children and clothed their crimes against humanity with all the elaboration of legend.

Blue Duck, however, is not finished with these two old Rangers. Woodrow F. Call is given the privilege of meeting Blue Duck while transporting McCrae's body back to Texas for burial. In Santa Rosa, New Mexico, Call visits Blue Duck in his cell, where he is awaiting execution on the gallows.

Call can find no pleasure in hanging men anymore, having found it necessary to hang his old friend, Jake Spoon, for, among other things, stealing horses. He can find no salve for the guilt of too many dawn raids on helpless noncombatants. In a fit of conscience he had refrained from massacring a small, starving band of Northern Indians who had stolen some of his horses for food, only to cause the death of his faithful Black scout. He found no joy in being the first man to bring cattle into Montana, having left the ranch in the hands of young Newt. But he will find pleasure in watching Blue Duck hang. Watching Blue Duck hang may be the last pleasure remaining to him in life.

But Blue Duck will not hang. As he is led from his cell he grabs the deputy who arrested him and plunges through a high window in the jail, hurtling himself and the deputy to their deaths on the ground below. He provides Call with a sharp contrast between his suicide, taking an enemy with him, and McCrae's lingering death, bribing a Montana whore to keep playing a piano until he is gone.

If Larry McMurtry's vision of the West, and the place of the Texas Rangers in it, had coincided with John Prebble's view of these men, the popular myth McMurtry retold might have become a cautionary tale. It might have told us that we must step outside the ethnocentricity of our culture and examine the methods by which we gain fame, and if they are grounded in squalor, so shall our souls be.

Works Cited

Arkeketa, Annette. Panel discussion, "Native Writing and Contemporary Native Issues." Returning the Gift: A Festival of

North American Native Writers. Norman, Oklahoma, 9 July 1992.

Cape, Lois, and Gordon Dedam. "Texas AIM Chapter Stages De-celebration Protest." *Micmac News* Sydney, Novia Scotia, Canada . July 1992: 20.

Clifford, Craig Edward. *In The Deep Heart's Core: Reflections on Life, Letters, and Texas.* College Station: Texas A&M UP, 1985.

———, and Tom Pilkington, eds. *Range Wars: Heated Debates, Sober Reflections, and Other Assessments of Texas Writing.* Dallas: Southern Methodist UP, 1989.

The Comancheros. Dir. Michael Curtiz. With John Wayne, Lee Marvin, and Stuart Whitman. Screenplay by James Grant and Clair Huffaker. Twentieth Century Fox, 1961. 107 min.

Curtis, Edward S. *The North American Indian.* Vol 19. New York: Johnson Reprint Corp., 1970. Orig. pub.,1930.

Cushman, H. B. *History of the Choctaw, Chickasaw, and Natchez Indians.* Ed. by Angie Debo. New York: Russel & Russel, 1972. Orig. pub., 1899.

Dugger, Ronnie, ed. *Three Men in Texas: Bedichek, Webb, and Dobie; Essays by Their Friends in the Texas Observer.* Austin: U of Texas P, 1967.

Everett, Dianna. *The Texas Cherokees: A People Between Two Fires, 1819–1840.* Norman: U of Oklahoma P, 1990.

Hud. Dir. Martin Ritt. With Paul Newman, Patricia Neal, Melvyn Douglas, and Brandon De Wilde. Screenplay by Irving Ravetch and Harriet Frank, Jr. Based on the novel *Horseman, Pass By,* by Larry McMurtry. Paramount, 1963. 112 min.

Hughes, W. J. *Rebellious Ranger: Rip Ford and the Old South-west.* Norman: U of Oklahoma P, 1964.

Lincecum, Gideon. "Life of Apushimataha." *Publications of the Mississippi Historical Society* 9 (1905–06) 415–85.

Little Big Man. Dir. Arthur Penn. With Dustin Hoffman, Faye Dunaway, Richard Mulligan, and Chief Dan George. Screen-play by Calder Willingham. Based on the novel by Thomas Berger. National General, 1970. 147 min.

Lonesome Dove. Dir. Simon Wincer. With Robert Duvall, Tommy Lee Jones, Danny Glover, Diane Lane, Robert Urich, Frederic Forrest, D.B. Sweeney, Rick Schroder, and Angelica Huston. TV mini-series in four parts: Pt. 1, Leaving; Pt. 2, On the Trail; Pt. 3, The Plains; Pt. 4, Return. Teleplay by Bill Wittlife. Based on the novel by Larry McMurtry. Cabin Fever Entertainment, 1991. Orig. TV release, 1989. 360 min.

McMurtry, Larry. "Southwestern Literature?" *In A Narrow Grave: Essays On Texas.* Albuquerque: U of New Mexico P, 1987. 31–54. Orig. pub.,1968.

————. *Lonesome Dove.* New York: Simon and Schuster, 1985.

Newcomb, W. W., Jr. *The Indians of Texas: From Prehistoric to Modern Times.* Austin: U of Texas P, 1961.

Nye, Wilbur Sturtevant. *Plains Indian Raiders: The Final Phase of Warfare from the Arkansas to the Red River.* Norman: U of Oklahoma P, 1968.

Prebble, John. *The Buffalo Soldiers.* New York: Bantam, 1964. Orig. pub., 1959.

Reynolds, Clay. *Taking Stock: A Larry McMurtry Casebook.* Dallas: Southern Methodist UP, 1989.

Richardson, Rupert Norval. *The Comanche Barrier to South Plains Settlement: A Century and a Half of Savage Resistance to the Advancing White Frontier.* Glendale: Arthur H. Clark, 1933.

————. *Texas: The Lone Star State.* 2nd ed. Englewood Cliffs: Prentice-Hall, 1958.

Samora, Julian, Joe Bernal, and Albert Pena. *Gunpowder Justice: A Reassessment of the Texas Rangers.* Notre Dame: U of Notre Dame P, 1979.

Scheuer, Steven H., ed. *Movies On TV.* 8th rev. ed. New York: Bantam, 977.

Shaw, Gary. *Meat On The Hoof: The Hidden World of Texas Football.* New York: Dell, 1973. Orig. pub., 1972.

Stedman, Raymond William. *Shadows of the Indian: Sterotypes in American Indian Culture.* Norman: U of Oklahoma P, 1982.

True Grit. Dir. Henry Hathaway. With John Wayne, Glen Campbell, Kim Darby, Robert Duvall, and Dennis Hopper. Screenplay by Marguerite Roberts. Based on the novel by Charles Portis. Paramount, 1969. 128 min.

Utley, Robert M. *Frontiersmen in Blue: The United States Army and the Indian, 1848–1865.* Lincoln: U of Nebraska P, 1981. Orig. pub., 1967.

Wallace, Ernest, and E. Adamson Hoebel. *The Comanches: Lords of the South Plains.* Norman: U of Oklahoma P, 1952.

Wilbarger, J. W. *Indian Depredations In Texas*. Austin: Steek Co.,
    1935. Orig. pub., 1889.
Webb, Walter Prescott. *The Great Frontier*. Austin: U of Texas P,
    1951.
_____. *The Texas Rangers: A Century of Frontier Defense*. With a
    Foreword by Lyndon Johnson. 2nd ed. Austin: U of Texas P,
    1965. Orig. pub., 1935.

The Great Prairie West
Of The Cross Timber
▼ ▼ ▼ ▼ ▼ ▼ ▼ ▼ ▼ ▼ ▼ ▼ ▼ ▼ ▼ ▼

Choctaws, and a select and rather curious assortment of
other Indian nations, glance at a calendar and note that the
agreement establishing and perpetuating peace and friendship among them, and securing to each of them free permission to hunt and trap in the "Great Prairie west of the
Cross Timber" (more commonly known as the southern
Great Plains), will mark its 165th anniversary in the year
2000.

Ever since August 24, 1835, when the great Comanche
horseman, Isacoly (the Wolf), stepped forward to be the
first of 186 Indians to put his signature on the Treaty of
Camp Holmes, the Comanches, Wichitas, Cherokees,
Muscogees, Choctaws, Osages, Senecas, and Quapaws, the
eight signatory Indian nations to the treaty (the ninth signatory nation being the Unites States), have cherished the
notion of "free permission" to hunt and trap in the southern Great Plains region.

This cherished notion was embodied formally in article
four of the treaty: "It is understood and agreed by all the
nations or tribes of Indians parties to this treaty, that each
and all of the said nations or tribes have free permission to
hunt and trap in the Great Prairie west of the Cross Timber;
to the western limits of the United States."

In the Treaty of Camp Holmes, which was orchestrated
by the United States, the United States purchased an easement guaranteeing its citizens a right of free passage
through the region (article three), and the eight signatory
Indian nations agreed to share the hunting and trapping

rights within the region. That sounds simple enough, and the treaty, on its face, appears to be a simple agreement. It is, however, an agreement of such complexity that only a lawyer could love it.

What happened at Camp Holmes depends upon one's point of view. One might assume, for example, that the Comanches and Wichitas, as residents of the region, exercising such attributes of sovereignty as are characteristic of nations of people in their homeland, were the ones who agreed to sell the easement through their homeland to the United States and that they were the ones who agreed to share their hunting and trapping rights within the region with the other six signatory Indian nations, who were in the process of being moved to new homes at the edge of the plains, and that the Comanches and Wichitas were willing to do this in consideration of "establishing and perpetuating peace and friendship" with the new arrivals, and in exchange for "presents," a "donation of the United States" (article eight). Historians insist upon reporting that this was, in fact, what happened.

Any self-respecting Choctaw, however, would scoff at such an account, and would be quick to point out that while the treaty is explicit about who is receiving what, it is silent about who is receiving what from whom, and that one must understand that what actually happened in the Treaty of Camp Holmes was that the United States purchased its easement through the homeland of the Comanches and Wichitas from the Choctaws and the Muscogees (Creeks), and that the Comanches and Wichitas were granted the right to hunt and trap within their own homeland by a combination of parties which included the Quapaws, the Choctaws, the Muscogees, and the United States. The Comanches and Wichitas, you see, did not own their own homeland.

It had been owned by the French, from whom the United States had purchased it in 1803 (the Louisiana Purchase); and if French title to the area had not been exclusive, then a huge portion amounting to most of the southern half of the region had been owned by the Quapaws, and the United States had purchased it from them in 1818 (by a transaction in which the Quapaws had reserved for themselves the right to hunt throughout that portion of the region), and a huge portion amounting to most of the northern half of the region had been owned by the Osages, and the United States had purchased it from them in 1825. This may seem as though the United States had been paying good money for the region to whoever happened to come along offering to sell it, but as any good Choctaw will tell you, the United States has a penchant for acting in strange and mysterious ways where land is concerned.

Comanches and Wichitas might not have been impressed by these purchases, had they known about them, considering that the Osages had lived for the most part a goodly distance away in what is today the state of Missouri, and the Quapaws had lived for the most part a goodly distance away in what is today the state of Arkansas, and the French lived all the way across an ocean. But the United States professed them to be valid titles to the land, and, as the Choctaws had learned by then, the opinion of the United States in such matters was what counted.

The United States had been selling these titles about as fast as it had been acquiring them, and, by 1835, had succeeded in creating a great confusion regarding legal claims of various sorts by various parties to various portions of the southern Great Plains, having sold a huge area in the southern portion of the region to the Choctaws in 1820 (a sale which was burdened by the prior reservation of the Quapaws to a share in the hunting rights throughout that portion of the region), and the United States had sold a large tract in the middle portion of the region to the Muscogees in 1832 and 1833, and the United States was on the verge of burdening a large tract in the northern portion of the region by a guarantee to the Cherokees of a "perpetual outlet west, and a free and unmolested use of all the country west of" the seven million acres that were to com-

prise the Cherokee Nation in what is today the northeastern corner of the state of Oklahoma (an agreement which
was completed by the end of the year and which undoubtedly accounted for the presence of the two Cherokee representatives who signed the Treaty of Camp Holmes).

The assembly at Camp Holmes was, therefore, a
landowner's convention *par excellence*, consisting of former, present, and future holders of various sorts of title to
various portions of the southern Great Plains, who were
meeting with representatives of some of the Plains Indians
who actually resided on the land, complicated by the ad-
mixture of the overshadowing presence of the United
States, which, despite having divested itself of title to
much of the region, maintained that it still had some sort
of supervisory authority even in those portions of the region which it no longer claimed to own, and which was responsible for serious stresses and anxieties between the
Plains Indians and the other Indians by having pushed the
six other signatory Indian nations right to the very borders
of the Comanche and Wichita homelands, and which was
attempting to intercede its good offices to try to orchestrate
some accommodation between the various parties, as well
as to secure for itself an easement in the form of a right of
passage through the region for its citizens, which it had ne-
glected to do when selling much of the region to the
Choctaws and the Muscogees, and to try to get the Comanches and Wichitas to honor this easement, apparently
by allowing them to think that it was being purchased from
them.

For the Comanches and Wichitas this was their first ex-
posure to the way in which the United States when about
doing things, and it doesn't appear that any of the partici-
pants at the assembly took the bother of trying to explain
any of the underlying complexities to them. After all, if it
should be the place of the Choctaws to help educate the
Plains Indians in the ways of civilization, then, considering that the Choctaws stood an excellent chance of eventually being declared the owner of much of the region, let the

lessons take place over a period of time where they might be most fully appreciated by the Comanches and Wichitas by means of hindsight.

The Choctaws understood well enough what was taking place at Camp Holmes, for they had already traveled the same road the Comanches and Wichitas were now setting themselves upon. At Camp Holmes the United States was formally and legally making the acquaintance of the Comanches and Wichitas, getting it down on paper that they were entering a period known as "peace and friendship," and making certain that the Comanches and Wichitas understood that citizens of the United States would now become an increasingly frequent sight in their neighborhood, by right of passage through their homeland, so that citizens of the United States could get to somewhere else, in this case to "the Mexican Provinces," where, one might assume, they had urgent and frequent business.

In 1786 the United States had gotten it down on paper that the Choctaws and the United States were entering into this period of "peace and friendship." In 1801 the United States had gotten it down on paper that they were asking and receiving permission to build a wagon road through the ancestral homeland of the Choctaws, and within thirty years of that date the Choctaws had found themselves on that road, dispossessed of all they had ever owned east of the Mississippi River.

Between the time the Choctaws had granted the United States an easement through their ancestral homeland in 1801 and the time they sat down at Camp Holmes in 1835 to negotiate their first treaty after having been removed to their new lands in the west (to the extreme eastern portion of those western lands, in present-day southeastern Oklahoma), something had happened that changed the nature of official business between the Choctaws and the United States; during that interim the Choctaws had educated themselves a lawyer.

His name was James Lawrence McDonald, who was a half-blood Choctaw. At the age of fourteen McDonald had been sent east to be a ward in the home of Colonel Thomas L. McKenney, who was a friend of Pushmataha, war chief of the Okla Hunnali division of the Choctaws (In 1816 McKenney had become Superintendent of Indian Trade; in 1824 he had organized the Bureau of Indian Affairs and had become its first chief). While living in McKenney's home, McDonald pursued a course of general educational instruction under the tutelage of the Rev. Dr. Carnahan (who later became President of Princeton College). McDonald was then sent to Ohio, where he read law in the office of Judge John McLean (who later became a Justice of the Supreme Court). After being admitted to the practice of law, McDonald returned to the Choctaw country, in what by then had become the east-central portion of the state of Mississippi, where he was appointed a member of the Choctaw delegation of 1824, which was led by Pushmataha, Puckshenubbee, and Moshulatubbee, the three district war chiefs of the Choctaws, which traveled to Washington, D.C. to negotiate the Treaty of Washington, dated January 20, 1825.

Though McDonald's legal skills had not been available to the Choctaws at Camp Holmes (McDonald had died by then), and were not needed, as Moshulatubbee and the thirty other Choctaw delegates were perfectly capable of attending to the business to be conducted at Camp Holmes, they had been desperately needed in 1824, and they had saved the Choctaws from losing much of what they had gained in the Treaty of 1820, and they had gained for the Choctaws significant benefits and payments for those portions of the Treaty of 1820 which the United States had sought to negate, as well as requiring that the United States settle many outstanding Choctaw claims of a wide variety before the Choctaws would entertain the notion of modifying the Treaty of 1820.

In 1824 Puckshenubbee had died on the way to Washington, D.C., Pushmataha had died after arriving there, and McDonald had taken charge of the negotiations and had taught the other members of the Choctaw delegation how to conduct business with the United States. Concerning the role of his former ward in these negotiations, the chief of the new Bureau of Indian Affairs, Thomas L. Mckenney, said, "I found him so skilled in the business of his mission . . . as to make it more of an up-hill business than I had ever before experienced in negotiating with Indians. I believe Mr. Calhoun thought so too."

James Lawrence McDonald was the first in a long succession of Choctaws who found formal training in the law to be a desirable and useful skill in conducting official business with the United States and in conducting the internal affairs of their own nation. From an early date, and throughout the duration of the Choctaw Nation, until Oklahoma statehood in 1907, the Choctaws placed great store in formal education, establishing their own schools, maintaining a Choctaw Academy in Kentucky until it was destroyed during the Civil War, and throughout the remainder of the century sending their most promising young people back east to be formally educated, often at Yale.

In 1820, in the Treaty of Doak's Stand, the Choctaws had concluded a huge land deal with the United States. For a portion of their ancestral homeland east of the Mississippi River (5,500,000 acres, subsequently divided into nine Mississippi counties), the Choctaws had received legal title to approximately eleven million acres west of the Mississippi River, encompassing portions of four present-day states, from south-central Arkansas, through southern Oklahoma below the Canadian River (South Canadian River), through the Texas panhandle between the Canadian and Red Rivers, and into northeastern New Mexico to the source of the Canadian River in the Rocky Mountains. At that time, this tract included a large portion of Spanish territory, to which the Mexican government had succeeded at the conclusion of the Mexican Revolution in 1821, and it also included the very heart of the Comanche, Kiowa, Kiowa Apache, and Wichita nations. The Choctaws, however, try as they might, were never able to find a volunteer to go break this news to their new Plains Indian tenants, and so, in 1830, in the

Treaty of Dancing Rabbit Creek, the Choctaws had been willing to give up their claims to any land lying west of the 100th meridian (which brought their western border into line with the western border of the United States in that area, as had been established by the Adams-Onis Treaty of 1819 between Spain and the United States). The 100th meridian is the present eastern border of the Texas panhandle, which left the Choctaws in legal possession of all of the Great Plains region of what is today the southwestern quarter of the state of Oklahoma, and which left the Choctaws with the problem of what to do about the hordes of Comanches and other Plains Indians who had yet to be informed that they were now vassals of the Choctaws.

By 1835 the Choctaws had themselves been removed to their western land and had settled in the extreme eastern portion of it, in the ten and one-half county area of the southeastern portion of the present state of Oklahoma, which constitutes the Choctaw Nation of Oklahoma today. In 1835, if anyone could be counted on to attend to this delicate matter regarding the Plains Indians it was surely the United States, and if the Comanches and Wichitas should be so foolish as to continue to expend their energies chasing buffalo, when they should be educating themselves some lawyers, it was not for the Choctaws to weep for them when the day came that the Comanches and Wichitas should learn the results of their folly.

Of all the parties represented at Camp Holmes, the Senecas were the only ones who had no apparent former, present, or future legal relationship with the southern Great Plains region, though they acquired a significant one at Camp Holmes in the form of hunting and trapping rights. The Senecas, being the so-called Senecas of Sandusky, a small group from Ohio which had broken away from the Senecas in the distant past, and which had absorbed and adopted so many remnant groups of Indians that they had long since ceased being Senecas, except in name, and even in this regard they were more commonly known as "Mingoes," were representative of the large number of Indian nations from many different parts of the continent which were soon to be removed to new homes adjacent to the "Great Prairie west of the Cross Timber," and for which some accommodation had to be made with the Plains Indians.

Further complicating matters at Camp Holmes was the fact that the Comanches and Wichitas who signed the treaty represented only a portion of their nations. Had the American commissioners not been delayed in their arrival at Camp Holmes the agreement would have included other groups of Plains Indians, for, as U.S. Army Assistant Surgeon Leonard McPhail attests in his diary, Kiowas and members of other branches of the Comanche Nation had been camped "within hail" until, weary of waiting for the American commissioners, and running out of food, they had left.

The Americans had first tried to get the Plains Indians to come to Fort Gibson, but the Plains Indians had insisted that the Americans and the eastern Indians come to them, and so the site of Camp Holmes had been agreed upon, near the edge of the plains, at the confluence of Little River and the Canadian River (the South Canadian), near present-day Holdenville, Oklahoma. Various elements of the U.S. Army had arrived at Camp Holmes piecemeal, and, early on, the Comanche chief "Ta-ba-que-na" had tried to induce his colleagues to wipe out the army encampment, but with the arrival of additional troops, and the firing of a "big gun," such plans were abandoned.

The Americans seriously underestimated the difficulties they would encounter in attempting to work their way through the Cross Timber and found that torrential rains, swollen rivers, ravines that were impassable for wagons until rude bridges had been constructed, steep creek banks that had to be cut before wagons could get down them, and a high rate of sickness among the troops from "prairie fever" all contributed to extended delays for the various units of the U.S. Army in making their way to Camp Holmes.

Given the array of legal claims to the region, in the aggregate, of all parties to the treaty, including those of the United States, the treaty certainly had the effect of burdening all future transactions regarding the land in question with a prior conveyance of hunting and trapping rights to the eight signatory Indian nations, as article four of the treaty is explicit in that regard. The nine signatory nations have never seen fit to reconvene an assembly for the purpose of modifying the treaty or revoking any of its provisions. Indeed, the assembly at Camp Holmes in 1835 is the only time in history when these specific nine nations have ever concluded a mutually binding agreement, one with another. Today, citizens of the United States still enjoy the right of free passage through the region, which was established for them by the treaty, and the signatory Indian nations still cherish the "free permission" to hunt and trap there. One might note, however, that officials of state governments within the region are not particularly well educated concerning this provision of the treaty.

We can say with some geographical precision where the Cross Timber can be found and what the natural borders are encompassing the "Great Prairie west of the Cross Timber." The Cross Timber is a great natural barrier of vegetation that borders the eastern edge of the southern Great Plains. It is composed primarily of post oak and blackjack oak. These trees grow so close together that the barrier was sufficient to hold the great herds of buffalo to the west of it. When the area first began to be settled it was nearly impossible to get a wagon through the barrier until a sufficient number of roads had been constructed. It was a barrier of such dimension and endurance that on either side of it the Indians were distinctly different, were descended from different language families and possessed different cultures.

Another characteristic of the Cross Timber at the time of settlement was that much of its low-lying areas consisted of a dense tangle of briars and thickets in the many river bottoms, river bottoms which today are largely buried beneath reservoirs. Constantly subject to flooding, with some of them bordered by sloughs and swamps, and with some of them consisting of treacherous mud bogs and quaking sandy flats, the river bottoms themselves were virtually impassable to wheeled vehicles and were dangerous on horseback.

The Cross Timber, was, simply, one of the great natural barriers on the earth. On today's maps it can be said to extend from southeastern Kansas, through east-central Oklahoma, and into north-central Texas. In Kansas and Texas the Cross Timber is a fairly narrow belt, but in Oklahoma it broadens to encompass about a third of the width of the state, extending into western Oklahoma in narrow belts along the bottomlands of rivers, and containing large islands of tall grass prairies throughout its reaches. It enters Oklahoma from Kansas in narrow belts in Washington County and Osage County in the northeast, spreads out over much of the eastern half of the state that is not a part of the Ozark Plateau, the Ouachita Mountains, the Arbuckle Mountains, or tall grass prairies, extends into east-central Arkansas along the bottomlands of the Arkansas River, abuts the Gulf Coastal Plain region of oak-hickory and loblolly pine forests in the extreme southeastern corner of Oklahoma, and enters Texas through six Oklahoma border counties, from the eastern end of Jefferson County to the western edge of McCurtain County. The very heart of the Cross Timber, therefore, is found in Oklahoma, and the very heart of the "Great Prairie west of the Cross Timber" is to be found in western Oklahoma, the Texas panhandle, and northeastern New Mexico, augmented by a significant strip of southern Kansas and southeastern Colorado, and a strip of north Texas below the Texas panhandle running from near interstate 35 to the New Mexico border.

This "Great Prairie west of the Cross Timber" is a huge region drained by many rivers, the Arkansas, the Cimarron, the Canadian, the Wichita, the Red, the upper Brazos, and the upper reaches of the Pecos among them. It includes large portions of five states, Oklahoma, Kansas,

Texas, Colorado, and New Mexico. Elevations range from near 1000 feet at the eastern edge to five or six thousand feet on the arid high plains along the western edge.

Oklahoma City sits approximately in the center of the north-south boundary, at the very western edge of the Cross Timber, or at the very eastern edge of the Great Plains, depending upon how you want to look at it; its western suburbs sit on the edge of the Great Plains; its eastern suburbs sit in the edge of the Cross Timber. Drive west from Oklahoma City along Interstate 40 and you are in the "Great Prairie west of the Cross Timber."

Some might be surprised to learn that the region played a vital role in the cultures of eastern Indians long before the removal of many eastern nations to lands west of the Mississippi River, and long before any white men stumbled upon the North American continent.

It might seem as though Indians from east of the Mississippi, such as the Choctaws, were relocated to lands adjacent to the Great Plains too late for their association with the region, especially with its teeming masses of buffalo, to be more than a footnote in their history. It might seem that the buffalo herds were, for the Choctaws, something that were available only for a short time, no more than about a generation, and that the region's great buffalo herds were something to which they were exposed as a sort of accident of history, and that its influence on their culture could only have been fleeting and superficial at best. Nothing could be further from the truth.

The region of the southern Great Plains played such an important role in Choctaw culture that authorities in Spanish Louisiana were continually vexed by problems in what is today Louisiana and east Texas, caused by troublesome Choctaws who traversed the area regularly by what they regarded as their ancestral right to seek adventure in the west. The ancient Choctaw homeland in present-day east-central Mississippi and western Alabama may seem a long way from northeastern New Mexico and the panhandle of Texas, yet Choctaws were intimately acquainted with the high plains region and were not bashful about demonstrating their familiarity with it.

In 1820, at the negotiations for the Treaty of Doak's Stand, Pushmataha, the Choctaw war chief, was openly contemptuous of U.S. Army maps of the region and of General Andrew Jackson's proposed western boundary for new Choctaw land west of the Mississippi, which Jackson was offering to swap to the Choctaws. Jackson had proposed that the boundary be set along a line running from the source of the Canadian River due south to Red River. Pushmataha took the handle of his pipe hatchet and traced a map for Jackson on the ground to demonstrate that a line running due south from the source of the Canadian River (in the front range of the Rockies) would strike no portion of Red River (whose headwaters are to be found on the high plains, east of the Pecos). Pushmataha further informed Jackson that such little water as there was in much of the vast region that Jackson was offering to swap was "bookie." It was not second-hand knowledge that Pushmataha was relaying, for he had spent much of his life in the region of the southern Great Plains, especially along its eastern fringes.

Because Pushmataha became a famous contemporary of men such as Tecumseh and Andrew Jackson, and because he became acquainted with literate men who would later write accounts of his life, such as the frontier physician and naturalist, Dr. Gideon Lincecum, and the first Chief of the Bureau of Indian Affairs, Colonel Thomas L. McKenney, we know a great deal about Pushmataha's early life and the manner in which he rose to a position of power among the Choctaws. He followed a traditional, time-honored path for young Choctaws out to prove themselves; he went west.

The buffalo plains were a magnet for eastern Indians, and not just for Choctaws. We know that Tecumseh, in his twentieth year, accompanying his older brother Chiksika and ten other Shawnees, spent an entire year with the Sacs at the edge of the northern Great Plains, and that they spent the entire fall hunting on the buffalo plains to the north and west in the lands of the Dakotahs, dodging Sioux war parties, marveling at the hundreds of thousands of animals, engaging in wild chases on horseback, and then drying the meat on racks for winter food before retreating to the northeast into the woodlands to spend the winter trapping.

A young Choctaw's first exploit to the southern plains would likely come at the conclusion of winter hunts for bear in the Louisiana bottoms. Rather than return to the Choctaw homeland across the Mississippi, having no family as yet to provide for, the young warrior was likely to join one of the parties forming up to continue on to the west. They would often be looking for adventure and hunting, rather than trouble, but just as often they would be looking for trouble, and even when not looking for it, it often came their way. The southern Great Plains provided a training ground and proving ground for young Choctaw warriors, a place to add the coveted "ubi" (or "ubbee," killer) to their name without disrupting Choctaw relations with other nations adjacent to their homeland. Pushmataha became one of those Choctaws who went looking for trouble.

Historians and ethnologists have consistently failed to realize the menace the Choctaws represented to people living west of the Mississippi River, especially to isolated, small bands they encountered on the southern Great Plains. The deep, bitter, and heavily documented hatred between Osages and Choctaws, for example, was not a result of any clashes between those two peoples in present-day Missouri or in present-day Mississippi, their ancestral homelands. They encountered one another on the plains, where both nations hunted and sought adventure. Fairly large, roving bands of young Choctaw hellions, even small groups, out to kill, unburdened by any women, any elderly, or any young, capable of striking and retreating quickly, terrorized the region of the southern Great Plains for centuries unknown. Their activities cast a hollow echo to descriptions of the Choctaws as "peaceable" or having an inclination to engage only in defensive warfare. Such characterizations, which one finds frequently in the literature regarding the Choctaws, are based entirely on the relations of the Choctaws with their neighbors in the southeast and take no account of the sudden terror of Choctaw aggression in the west, where young Choctaws received their instruction in warfare.

It has been said that the young Pushmataha distinguished himself to such an extent on a winter bear hunt in the Louisiana bottoms that he became an object of much curiosity to older, more experienced warriors, who invited him to join them on an expedition to the west. The thing that held the interest of the men, other than his complete lack of fear, bordering on a complete lack of common sense, in attacking wounded, cornered, enraged bears with a spear, was his unrestrained bragging. They named him "Ishtilawata" (the braggart, not an entirely flattering name in Choctaw culture). In the west, in a day-long fight, he disappeared early in the contest and was not seen again until he arrived at the rendezvous point near midnight. The men ridiculed him for cowardice, until he opened a pouch and threw four or five fresh scalps on the ground, which he had taken in a single-handed onslaught at the enemy's rear. He is then reported to have said, "Let him laugh who can show more scalps." From that day forward, having come from complete obscurity, his rise was rapid.

He became one of those who, having been to the west, drummed up expeditions of his own, and it was one of his earliest expeditions, perhaps the very first one that he led, perhaps the second or third, that met with disaster. Caught by surprise in an ambush, Pushmataha was one of the only ones, perhaps the only one, who escaped. The experience changed his life.

Rather than seek adventure in the west for a time during his youth, prove himself as a warrior, and then turn to other pursuits, he seethed with hatred and a desire for revenge. Some accounts say that he spent as many as three to five years in the west after his defeat, living for a time with the Spanish, studying the habits of his enemies, and learning their seasonal movements, before he returned to the Choctaw country to drum up another expedition. He became obsessed with leading expeditions to the west until his reputation had grown to such an extent that he became the most powerful war chief in the nation, able, by sheer force of will, to prevent the Choctaws from joining Tecumseh's pan-Indian alliance, in a series of face to face debates with Tecumseh in the Choctaw country in 1811.

Practically every contemporary of Pushmataha's who provided information to his biographers identified a different nation of Indians in the west as his main enemy. He evidently had many enemies in the west. Peter Perkins Pitchlynn, who as a young man had known Pushmataha, and who later became principal chief of the Choctaw Nation, told Charles Lanman that one of Pushmataha's expeditions suffered several Choctaws killed and that Pushmataha himself lost his favorite cap, ornamented with rattlesnake rattles and eagle feathers, when his party of one hundred Choctaws were attacked near the headwaters of the Red River by a large party of about five hundred Tonkawas. Of all the nations mentioned in various accounts, the one mentioned most often are the Osages.

There can be no doubt that Pushmataha had a deep and abiding enmity for the Osages. His most famous expedition in the west, and the one most heavily documented, was against the Osages. It resulted in voluminous testimony before the Congress of the United States.

When Pushmataha learned, in 1806, that a French trader named Joseph Bougie, from Arkansas Post near the mouth of the Arkansas River, was proceeding up the Arkansas in boats heavily laden with $10,000 worth of trade goods for the Osages, Pushmataha struck swiftly to prevent the goods from being distributed. Leaving present-day east-central Mississippi with a large party of Choctaw warriors, he attacked Bougie's trading post upstream on the Vertigris River, just above the Three Forks of the Arkansas (not far from present-day Tulsa, Oklahoma), scattered the Osages who had been escorting Bougie (without harming any white men), confiscated the entire supply of goods, and made off with it downriver in Bougie's boats, leaving Bougie and his men with no recourse but to appeal to Congress for compensation for their loses. After conducting hearings on the matter and taking testimony from witnesses who had been there, trading under license from the United States, the Congress eventually compensated Bougie for a portion of his claims.

The importance of the west to Pushmataha's career can scarcely be exaggerated, though it was undoubtedly an influence in his life to a much greater extent than to most Choctaws. Nevertheless, it is illustrative of the importance of the region to Choctaw culture, a place where men could seek adventure, and gain advancement as a direct result of those adventures, though the region was many hundreds of miles from the ancestral Choctaw homeland.

It was no accident of history that the Choctaws acquired legal title to much of the southern Great Plains region in 1820 from the United States. The United States, at President Thomas Jefferson's insistence, had been pressuring the Choctaws to move to the west ever since the negotiations for the Treaty of Mount Dexter in 1805, which undoubtedly caused Pushmataha to look at the west in a way he had never looked at it before, and which probably accounts for the marked intensity of Choctaw military expeditions to the west which are evident in the historical record in the years immediately following the Treaty of Mount Dexter. These have generally been interpreted as campaigns against the Osages, and there is certainly indisputable evidence that some of them were against the Osages, such as the previously mentioned attack on Bougie's trading post, but it is possible that aggressive and ruthless Choctaw military onslaughts were in part responsible for the complete depopulation of Caddoan peoples in the area now comprising southeastern Oklahoma, though Osage aggression and devastating smallpox epidemics have usually been advanced to explain why the Choctaws found an empty land awaiting them upon their removal, despite tantalizing suggestions in the historical record that the Choctaws may have been responsible for providing themselves with their own home in the west.

By 1835, at Camp Holmes, when the Choctaws sat in council for the first time with their Plains Indian tenants, the Choctaw homeland was no longer hundreds of miles distant from the plains, but right next door, and Choctaw interest in the plains region had quickened. In 1855 the Choctaws were able to begin collecting a rather substantial rent for their holdings on the Great Plains, in the form of a $600,000 payment from the United States for a lease from the Choctaws for land lying between the 98th and 100th meridians, to provide a home for the Wichitas and "such other tribes of Indians as the Government may desire to locate there." The area became known as the Leased District. The Chickasaws also received a $300,000 payment from the United States in this agreement, as the Choctaws had shared their holdings in the west with the Chickasaws upon the removal of the Chickasaws to the west, in an attempt to reunite to the two nations, which anciently had been one people, an attempt that failed.

Choctaws eventually surrendered title to the Leased District to the United States, for a payment of $300,000, in a treaty in 1866, leaving them as their only property interest in the southern Great Plains the "free permission" to hunt and trap in the "Great Prairie west of the Cross Timber" from the Treaty of Camp Holmes, an interest that includes a much larger area than the region for which the Choctaws had held a claim of outright ownership.

By 1866 the great herds of buffalo, the principal attraction for hunters in the region, were entering their decline. Their end would come so swiftly as to stagger the imagination. But the Great White Father, in his infinite wisdom, desired that the provisions of the treaty of Camp Holmes should be perpetual, that they "shall be obligatory on the nations or tribes parties hereto from and after the date hereof, and on the United States from and after its ratification by the Government thereof" (article ten), even though neither the United States, nor the state of Oklahoma, has done a very good job of educating the farmers and ranchers in the region that their land is burdened by a prior reservation of the hunting and trapping rights. Most of the farmers and ranchers in the area think in terms of "ownership" the land they reside on. They are sophisticated enough to comprehend that their land can be burdened by a prior conveyance of the mineral rights, and that owners of the mineral interest can contract with oil and gas exploration companies, who can come onto their land and drill for oil and gas, without making any compensation to the residents, and that they can do so whether they like it or not. But the notion that Indians might still have some rights on their place usually draws nothing but a blank stare. The state of Oklahoma never freely acknowledges any restrictions on its powers where Indians are concerned until forced to acknowledge some remaining vestige of tribal sovereignty by the courts.

A few years ago, being a member of the Choctaw Nation, I found myself exercising my right to hunt on the Great Prairie West of the Cross Timber. It is a cold winter day, one that is clear and crisp and devoid of the bitter wind that usually blows here. Well north of a ranch house I have left a county road and walked about a half mile to a place along the rim of a small canyon where I can see the terrain below very well. The little creek bottom is choked with brush, but there are openings here and there, and directly beneath me is a long barren stretch. I sit on a rock at the edge of the rim, with a cedar tree behind me breaking up my silhouette, and I can see for a great distance all around, rolling, barren hills separated by brushy little creeks. I am on a portion of the Great Plains to which the Muscogees held legal title from the United States when the Muscogees and my Choctaw ancestors sat in council at

Camp Holmes and agreed to share hunting and trapping rights within the region.

My Choctaw companions have driven more than a mile to the north, where a county road crosses the little creek. They'll park there and work their way toward me. If there are deer along the creek, they might flush them down my way and I might get a shot.

On a quiet, cold, sunny afternoon there is time to sit and look and think, time to remember generations of ancestors who came to these plains, who, at great risk, came hundreds and hundreds of miles to see for themselves the teeming herds of buffalo, the deer, elk, antelope, and the wolves, coyotes, and grizzly bears. It required a great deal of effort for them to get here. Now there is easy access to the plains for anyone from anywhere and about all that is here are deer, coyotes, and cattle. Rather than being someplace where men strive to go, it is a place to drive across as quickly as possible while going somewhere else.

I have been sitting at the rim of the canyon for quite some time when I see a flash in the brush down along the creek. A moment later I see another flash, and then another.

It's a coyote, a large one with a full, thick coat of yellow fur, who comes loping out into an opening. The fur is prime, and my thoughts turn from eating venison to skinning this coyote. He is not alarmed and not in any great hurry, but he's not lingering along the way either. If he would stop and look back up the creek I would take the shot, a good one, but he doesn't stop and his course will bring him much closer.

As if playing, he bounds back and forth from one side of the little creek to the other, and I can see that he is even larger than I had thought. When he has drawn nearly even with me down below, and when I have him in my sights, leading him ever so slightly as I swing the barrel along, compensating for the angle, so as not to shoot over him, slowing my lead until the coyote is just about to overtake the spot I am aiming at, right in front of his chest, and when I am already beginning to apply pressure to the trigger, about to touch off the shot, the coyote suddenly changes direction, making a tremendous bound straight toward me, landing high up on the steep wall of the canyon, where he bounds again, and then again, changing direction slightly with each bound to land in places where there is just enough footing to keep going. In three or four bounds he negotiates the steepest portion of the canyon wall, which brings him to a level where he can continue upward by a series of switchbacks, which he takes at a fast trot, occasionally bounding again to reach a higher level.

I have frozen in position from the moment the coyote first began to climb the canyon wall, my rifle still aimed at the canyon floor. His course will bring him to a ledge about fifteen feet directly beneath me, and a little to the left, where he will either stop and look back up the creek or pad softly by. I can see now that the ledge runs off to my left, passes behind a small boulder, and then emerges at my level, a little further to the left, as a shallow depression, a natural highway for the coyote and one he has undoubtedly traveled many times. He will follow that little gully on to the top of the hill and cross over to the next little watershed, confident in his knowledge that my companions never even got a glimpse of him.

To take the shot when he will be directly below me on the ledge would require shifting my position. But to get him when he comes out from behind the boulder, at my level, when he will be broadside at close range, will mean only swinging the rifle barrel around, silently, during the moment when the boulder is between us. So I wait, frozen, and watch.

It takes only a few moments for the coyote to reach the ledge below me. With the climb behind him, he goes padding softly by, eyes straight ahead, in no hurry, a look of mirthful satisfaction on his face.

His trot carries him behind the boulder, and my rifle barrel swings silently. By the time the third second has ticked away I know that the big, yellow coyote will never emerge from behind the boulder into my rifle sights. I lower the rifle, knowing now why the coyote was grinning; he was grinning at me.

D. L. Birchfield, a member of the Choctaw nation of Oklahoma, has established himself in the last few years as one of Native America's brightest new voices. This first book of essays, chosen as co-winner of the prestigious North American Native Authors First Book Award, shows us why. These "Oratorical Choctologies," as the author calls them, range from the serious to the satirical, from incisive essay to poignant autobiography. Whether describing a  landmark Native authors gathering or bringing the cultural and historical landscape of Indian Oklahoma into brilliant focus, his work is always intelligent, entertaining, and as sharp as the bite of the prairie winds.

D. L. Birchfield was general editor of the eleven-volume *Encyclopedia Of North American Indians*, associate editor of *Durable Breath: Contemporary Native American Poetry*, and guest co-editor of the Native American literature special issue of *Callaloo* (University of Virginia and Johns Hopkins University Press). A graduate of the University of Oklahoma College of Law and a member of the Choctaw Nation of Oklahoma, he teaches American Indian Studies at Cornell University in the English Department, the History Department, and the Department of Rural Sociology and has taught in the Native American Studies Department at the University of New Mexico. He is a former editor of *Camp Crier* at the Oklahoma City Native American Center. In 1996 he was one of seven Cornell faculty to win a university-wide faculty paper proposal competition.

In 1988 he won a national award from the Chess Journalists of America. He is a member of the editorial staff for *Roundup* magazine (Western Writers of America), *Moccasin Telegraph* (Wordcraft Circle of Native Writers & Storytellers), *Studies in American Indian Literatures* (University of Richmond), *The Raven Chronicles* (independent literary quarterly, Seattle, WA), and the *Native Americas* quarterly journal (Cornell University).